POWER BI

A Complete Step-by-Step Guide for Beginners in Understanding Power Bi

Eric Scott

© Copyright 2019 Eric Scott - All rights reserved.

This document is geared towards providing exact and reliable information in regards to the topic and issue covered. The publication is sold with the idea that the publisher is not required to render accounting, officially permitted, or otherwise, qualified services. If advice is necessary, legal or professional, a practiced individual in the profession should be ordered.

- From a Declaration of Principles which was accepted and approved equally by a Committee of the American Bar Association and a Committee of Publishers and Associations.

In no way is it legal to reproduce, duplicate, or transmit any part of this document in either electronic means or in printed format. Recording of this publication is strictly prohibited and any storage of this document is not allowed unless with written permission from the publisher. All rights reserved.

The information provided herein is stated to be truthful and consistent, in that any liability, in terms of inattention or otherwise, by any usage or abuse of any policies, processes, or directions contained within is the solitary and utter responsibility of the recipient reader. Under no circumstances will any legal responsibility or blame be held against the publisher for any reparation, damages, or monetary loss due to the information herein, either directly or indirectly.

Respective authors own all copyrights not held by the publisher.

The information herein is offered for informational purposes solely, and is universal as so. The presentation of the information is without contract or any type of guarantee assurance.

The trademarks that are used are without any consent, and the publication of the trademark is without permission or backing by the trademark owner. All trademarks and brands within this book are for clarifying purposes only and are the owned by the owners themselves, not affiliated with this document.

Table of Contents

Introduction 1

Chapter 1: An Introduction to Power Bi 3

Chapter 2: Sharing Your Dashboard 21

Chapter 3: A Look at Data Refresh 38

Chapter 4: Using Power BI Desktop 52

Chapter 5: Retrieving Data from Services and Content Packs 70

Chapter 6: Building Data Models 85

Chapter 7: Improving Your Power Bi Reports 102

Conclusion 127

References 130

Introduction

First of all, I would like to thank you for taking the time to read "Power Bi: A Complete Step by Step Beginners Guide to Understanding Power Bi". An incredibly powerful tool, Power BI comes from the Microsoft stable and is an amazing tool aimed at business users.

Data is everywhere and businesses generate the vast majority of it. Gathering up all this digital information is one thing; understanding it and making sense of it is another thing entirely and that is where tools like Power Bi come to the rescue.

Power Bi is the name of an umbrella that covers a multitude of on-premises and cloud-based services and apps that all help a business to collate their data from various sources, manage it and analyze it, all through a simple, easy to use interface.

With Power Bi at your fingertips, you can pull all your data into one place, process it, and gain intelligent insights, using visual elements such as graphs and charts. With this, you can create and produce compelling reports that you can share with others in your organization.

With Power Bi, you can connect to various data sources, be it a basic spreadsheet in Excel to a complex database, in the cloud or on-premise. Based on the data you provide it, Power Bi will find insights by connecting to the data, cleaning it up, so it can be better understood and producing a series of visuals and reports that tell you, no just what is happening in your organization now, but what has happened before and what is to come. Because Power Bi uses machine learning algorithms, it can find patterns in your data, and make predictions on what could be, allowing you to produce forecasts so your organization is better prepared to meet the future.

I have aimed this guide at beginners, at people who don't know what Power Bi can do for them and their organization. With Power Bi, you can feed in vast amounts of data, far more than many other platforms can handle, and use some powerful algorithms to analyze it and spot trends. You can customize your reports, and set up KPI alerts so you are always up to date on the important measurements and metrics, all in one user-friendly environment.

Interested?

Please keep in mind that this guide is just the first step on a long journey in understanding and using Power Bi to its best capabilities. Although I have provided some examples to help you understand Power Bi, you should follow the guide using your own data as it will help you to understand it better.

If you are ready to learn, let's take the first step on our Power Bi journey.

Chapter 1

An Introduction to Power Bi

Meet Donald. He works for Corus as a budgeting manager. Corus is an electronics retailer with several global shops and an online shop. Each locations manager is responsible for providing Donald with their budget forecast for the following year. Donald puts all these forecasts together to come up with an overall forecast for his manager.

In October 2018, Donald starts work on the budgets for 2019. He uses an Excel workbook to produce this budget and he uses PowerPoint to create a presentation, which is shared with others in the organization. Donald decides that, this time, he wants to do something different. He wants to use Power Bi to produce his reports.

Throughout this entire guide, we will follow Donald as he learns about Power Bi, about how he can use it for building a reporting system for his budgets. What we won't do is dive into the complexities involved in building a budget as that is not what this guide is about. We will be focusing on what Power Bi can do for Donald in terms of his budgets.

While you are more than welcome to use the data examples I use, I do encourage you to use your own data. Don't focus on the examples too much in the guide; instead, focus your attention on learning how to use Power Bi for your own data. All the operations I show you can be used with any data so you can learn the tools while getting useful insights into your specific data.

Getting Started

As with any journey, it cannot begin until you take the first step. Let's take that step with Donald

Donald has got an Excel report showing the last three years of sales, divided into regions brands, and month. Corus sales are brand-oriented with some more seasonal than others – Donald needs to take these seasonal effects into account. To do this, he groups sales data by month.

Each year, Donald uses these numbers to make considerations, sharing them with the regional managers. They then provide their figures for the following year in the form of an Excel Workbook. He attends lots of meetings while computing the figures, with each manager bringing their own versions of the Workbook, their own calculations, and Donald wants a better way of streamlining the process.

That's where Power Bi comes in. Donald head about and wants to try it. He heard it could help him to create a collaborative environment so all those involved in the budgeting process can share their findings and work together.

He goes to www.powerbi.com to see what it's all about. Clicking on the Get Started Free button, he has to decide between Power Bi Desktop and Power Bi. There isn't much difference between them; the only real difference is that Power Bi Desktop is a desktop application while Power Bi is cloud-based and used via a web browser. You can do pretty much the same with both and they each complement one another perfectly.

Donald decides that Power Bi Desktop is for the more advanced tasks and opts to use the cloud0based Power Bi instead. He clicks Sign Up and is invited to create an account. Because he already has an Office 365 account, all he needs to provide is his email address. Rather than signing in with no additional steps, he goes back to the home page and clicks on Sign In"; providing his Office 365 details, he is treated to his first view of the portal.

Uploading Data

He wants to upload an Excel Workbook so he can see what Power Bi has to offer. The data is on his laptop in a local file so he clicks the Get button under Files. He is presented with several options – Ill discuss these in more detail later – and clicks on Local File. He finds the file he wants to load and clicks on Open. In just a few seconds, the file is uploaded to Power Bi.

Before I go further, let's just look at the organization in the Power Bi portal. On the left, you see a pane called My Workspace where you will see:

- **Dashboards** – shows all your created dashboards. When you load a Workbook, Power Bi will create a dashboard, naming it the same as the uploaded file.

- **Reports** – shows the reports based on your own data

- **Datasets** – all the data sources that you have connected

Power Bi is about getting insights from your data. You start with one dataset and build some reports based on the data contained in it. Lastly, you draw up visualizations of those reports, turning them into dashboards. As you work through this guide, you will learn how to do all this. First, the basic operations.

Right now, Donald's dashboard only contains the file he uploaded and an option to Ask a Question. The file indicates that his Workbook is connected to his dashboard.

Natural-Language Queries

Power Bi allows you to ask plain English questions of your data to analyze it. This is called a natural-language query and you can use it to ask Power Bi to do tasks without needing any special syntax.

To see how it works, Donald types in "show sales 2018 by brand". Power Bi can understand this and shows Donald a bar chart; the brands are in alphabetical order and the bar length indicates the sales per brand for 2018.

As well as understanding what Donald wanted, Power Bi also showed him other queries while he was typing. The analysis showed that he could also look at the sales data by region and by month too and Power Bi gave him those suggestions.

Beside the question box is a pushpin; clicking that pins the visualization to the dashboard, allowing Donald to see it whenever he connects to Power Bi. Click it and you will see a Pin to Dashboard dialog box; click on Pin and the bar chart is pinned to the dashboard.

This is an impressive feature but is just one of the myriad of features you can use for analyzing your data.

Quick Insights

Quick Insight is a feature that allows Power Bi to look for data patterns and show a list of charts you can look at to understand your data better. Activating it is simple; click on the ellipsis on the right side of the dataset that you want to analyze – in our case, it would be 2018 sales data. The dataset menu opens, click on Quick Insights and the button will change to read View Insights.

When you run Quick Insight for the first time on any dataset, an analysis of the dataset is scheduled by Power Bi. This could take seconds or minutes; that depends on the size of the database. When it has finished, Power Bi will tell you that the search is finished.

This must be repeated whenever the data is updated but, while the data stays the same you can see the insights immediately.

What, exactly, are the insights?

Power Bi analyzes your data using artificial intelligence, looking for patterns in the data using sophisticated algorithms whose speed is dependent on the dataset complexity and size. On small datasets, like Donald's sales data, it doesn't take long to find the insights and once found, you have immediate access. Click on the Insights are Ready box and then on View Insights. The first two insights found will be shown; to see all of them, just scroll down the list.

The first insight shows Donald that most of the sales in the brand called A. Datum come from the USA and the second insight shows that both Corus and Adventure Works see a significant seasonal increase in sales for March.

Power Bi has no knowledge of your business nor of the economic scenario when it gathers your insights, so there could be any number of reasons why you get the findings that you do. Power Bi may be powerful but it is not a replacement for your brain, at least not where number interpretation comes in. But, with the use of those algorithms, it can easily find interesting points in your data.

Browsing is the best way to make use of insights. You can look for confirmation of things that you already know as well as new ideas. Not all the insights will always be that meaningful but, because

Power Bi will find so many of them, it's highly likely that you will find some jewels amongst them.

To enlarge an insight, just click it. Hover the mouse over one and you will see the pushpin; click it to pin that insight to your dashboard – if you have more than one dashboard, you can choose which one to pin it to.

When you pin an insight, you make it more interesting. You can resize or move any pinned visualization using a built-in grid, setting them how you want them.

Introducing Reports

Up to now, we have only made use of automated report building, using both Quick Insights and natural language queries. That really is only scratching at the surface of what Power Bi can do for you with reports. You can choose to manually build your reports and this will unleash Power Bi's full visualization capabilities.

This is easy to do; in the navigation pane, go to Datasets and click on any dataset – well use 2018 Sales. An empty report opens, showing you a very powerful interface. Powerful because one single window has multiple features. To the left is the standard navigation pane; the center pane is your reports canvas, where you add visualizations to build the report and configure the visualization properties. To the right there are two panes – Fields and Visualizations. The latter shows you all the visualizations available at the top and there are filtering options at the bottom. In the Fields pane, you can see all the dataset fields. Look at the individual columns in the Fields pane, you will see some have icons beside them – this indicates the main use of that field. If you use sales data for previous years, for example, 2015, 2016, and 2017, the icon will indicate summarization – each columns totals will be shown in any report they are used in. CountryRegion is indicated by a globe, telling you that geographical data is included and can be used for drawing data on a map.

Creating a report is easy – choose which fields you want in it. Donald chooses data for Sale 2018 and Brand. The brand has no summarization icon so, instead, it is used for slicing data. The Sales 2018 field does have the icon so the sum will be shown for the column.

When you do this, you create a default visualization – a grid showing the fields you are including with raw numbers. While the numbers are interesting, there is no indication of the relationship that exists between them. At first glance, Donald can't even see which of the brands is most important, which are the smallest, even the relative importance of any of the numbers. Charts give you a much clearer view and you can understand them quicker.

A tiles visualization can be modified simply by picking any of the chart types in Visualizations. For example, if you wanted a column chart, you would click on the visualization and then click the icon for the column chart. Do that with a dataset and you will find the numbers so much easier to read and understand.

You now know how to create a chart but one on its own is not a full report. Click an empty space on the center pane and repeat these steps to add different fields. Donald chooses to add the CountryRegion field and the Sale 2018 field and this generates another tile showing a map that has the sales in the regions contained in the dataset.

Maps are incredibly powerful tools but you need more than a few values. This provides a lot of detail but all you want is the relative size of the areas. That's where the column chart excels and the map can be transformed into one. You can then arrange your charts in your report.

As you can see, reports are nothing more than a collection of visuals, arranged in a way that communicates insights about your data. You should be able to see very clearly what is going on – with Donald's report, he can see that the USA, Germany and China all have roughly the same sales and that just a few brands make up the bulk of the sales.

Visual Interactions

This isn't too dissimilar from what could have been achieved just using an Excel spreadsheet and a pivot table or two on top of the sales tables. There are, however, a few differences between a report in Excel and the same report in Power Bi. Again, as you work through, I will discuss these differences but first, we'll look at the interactivity of a Power Bi report.

This feature is very similar to what Donald could have achieved by using Excel and a couple of pivot tables on top of the table containing sales, yet there are some important differences between a report created in Excel and the same report done by using Power BI. We will look at those as you proceed through the book, but, for the moment, let's look at the interactive nature of Power BI reports.

I'm going to choose the column titled Germany in the top chart. Whenever you click on a chart element, the report gets filtered and, in my case, I see how Germany contributed to all the sales of the brands – this is done through shading in two colors.

From this, Donald can see, very easily, Northwind in Germany shows small sales compared to the USA and China. That tells him that the brand is not popular in Germany and Donald now wants to know if the sales volumes in China and the US are equal or if one sells more than the other.

Donald clicks Northwind bar to see this analysis and the filter moves to the Brand from Country/Region. The Country/Region chart now highlights Northwinds contributions to the total sales figure.

The chart containing the sales by region shows Donald that most of the sales are in the USA but this is only a small brand so the chart isn't very clear in terms of sales importance between the different regions.

Before we carry on, it's time to get more accuracy in how we describe what we see. All charts will produce a visualization of the underlying numbers and any or all of them can act as a filter that you activate just by clicking on the chart. We saw filters a while ago; when we apply a filter to a chart it will highlight the contribution made by the filtered item to the grand total using two different shades of color. This feature is called visual Interaction ad it is quite interesting. There are, however, scenarios, much like the one that Donald is playing with right now, where it is better to compare, for example, the regional differences rather than the contribution made by one brand over the others.

Visual interactions can be precisely configured; in particular the filtering can be configured on a chart in terms of how it behaves against the other ones. We are using just two charts at the moment and that makes it ideal for experimenting with. Simply go the top menu bar on your report and click on Visual Interactions. Now, each chart shows different icon sets. The chart selected has the standard selection icon while the others display the three interaction types you can choose from:

1. The first is a funnel icon for filtering. Clicking on this filters the selected chart with the same filter on your destination chart. In this case, you do not see what contribution was made to the total; you only see the chart selection without values that relate to items not selected.

2. The second is the pie chart, showing the relative contribution. This is the default behavior and filtering on the

selected chart shows the relative contribution to the destination chart.

3. The third indicates no filtering interaction and when you filter one chart, it has no effect on the destination chart.

For example, if Donald selected the first one, filtering, on the brand sales to region sales chart, selecting Northwind would show another result on the resulting report. When you browse through the report, clicking on a brand shows you the highest-selling region – the insights are much clearer.

Decorating Reports

Donald has analyzed his data and now thinks that, although his report is simple, it does have some insights that he wants to share. He could screenshot it and share it in an email with a short description but Power Bi makes it easier than that by allowing him to annotate the report.

He could add some text, and shapes if he wanted. He could, for example, put a colored arrow on Northwind and add a text box with a few remarks about the findings; the report will be much easier to read.

Adding text is easy; click on Text Box above the center pane and type in your text, formatting it as you want it. Add the arrow by clicking on Shapes and then on Arrow. Move the arrow where you want it and resize it.

You do need to set properties for the text box and arrow objects. Simply click the object in the center pane and you will see all the properties appear in Visualizations.

Donald wants to rotate the arrow so he clicks it, goes to the Format shape window on the right and clicks Rotation. Then he drags the slider and changes the color of it too.

Lastly, bear in mind that any visual filters you set on the report are not saved as a part of that report. As such, when you go back to the chart, the arrow will tell you where the filter should be applied so you can see the data. Later, we'll look at permanent filters.

Saving Reports

Donald can now save his report and go back to it later. To do this, click File>Save and give it a name – Donald calls his Northwind. Once saved it shows in the My Workspace pane under Reports and Donald can access it whenever he goes into Power Bi. When you click a report to open it, you must activate it if you want to edit it, otherwise it stays as read-only. To activate, click Edit Report.

This is a good way of stopping changes being made unintentionally – you can see saved reports at any time but you must activate it if you want to make any changes.

Pinning Reports

When a report is opened in read-only, you will see a number of options along the top bar. You can save a copy, giving it another name, you can print it, edit it or apply other visualizations and more. One that is worth a mention is called Pin Live Page.

Where does this differ from pinning visualizations? When you do that, it is saved exactly as it is but the visualization won't be connected to any other in the dashboard. As such, there are no visual interactions between visualizations in a dashboard. This is a good thing because the dashboard isn't meant for interaction; to get that, simply click a visualization and open the source report.

However, on occasion, you will want to retain the visual interactions between some dashboard components. If you do, the report needs to be built and pinned as a whole as a live page. That way, any visualizations that belong to that page will maintain the visual interaction behavior although limited to those visuals in the pinned report.

In other words, any visualizations on the same report may interact between themselves whereas, when you filter it has no effect on any other visualization in that dashboard. For example, Donald has added the Northwind report to the dashboard; both charts are now mutually interactive but they have no effect on any other visualization in that dashboard and no other visualization will affect those in the report.

Refreshing Your Budget Workbook

Donald now has a basic understanding of Power BI and he has learned some useful insights that he can share with his managers.

However, before he can go any further, he wants to know how, when he has new figures, he can refresh his data. New forecasts will come in from his managers on a regular basis and these need to be added to the workbook. How can he upload this data to refresh what is already there?

Power Bi offers several ways to refresh data.

Donald gets his figures in a simple format – each manager sends a Workbook containing forecasts based on brand; they do not include monthly details.

Because these forecasts are at yearly level, but Donald's has his data at the monthly level, he goes for the simplest solution – the yearly sales are divided by 12 and the result copied to his Workbook in a column named Budget.

It is clear from the numbers that perhaps a different allocation should have been used because there is no seasonal reflection of any of the sales and, perhaps even more important, the figures are not right. Later, we will use another technique but, for now, we'll focus on what Power Bi has to offer and not on the budgeting figures.

The workbook on Donald's laptop has got different numbers and it is structured differently because it has the new Budget column. The Workbook in Power Bi still has all the old values and structure.

The easiest way would be to upload the new Workbook to Power Bi so Donald follows the same steps he did right at the beginning.

However, before the upload completes, Power Bi will throw up a warning telling him that there is already a dataset with this name. If he replaces the dataset with the new one, he might lose any changes made to the existing one. He hasn't made any changes so Donald just clicks Replace it and the old Workbook gets replaced with a new one.

Nothing was lost so Donald can continue. Now the new model in Power Bi has all the new data and the new column. As an aside, each report can have several pages so different visualizations can be added as and when he wants. This means that he can create a new report page, for example, and both will have different methods for visual interaction. It is common to add several copies of one visualization with different interactions and you are encouraged to make good use of it.

To make things clearer, Donald has given the visualizations different titles and has used a different font size too. On the right side, you will see a brush icon; click this to manage your visualization details.

Filtering Reports

You learned about visual interactions to make report filtering very easy but they do have limitations:

- Filters are not saved with the report; when you open reports, you can play with the visual filters but you cannot store them in the report you saved.

- Filters are always visible; you might want a filter for the whole report but you won't want any visual indication that the filter has been applied. That is a hidden filter that works in the background.

Power Bi offers you another way in the form of standard filters than can be applied to no less than three layers:

- **Visual-level** – these work on single visualizations and reduce the data that can be seen by the visualizations. They work on data and on calculations

- **Page-level** – these work on the report page level and you can have different filters for different pages in one report

- **Report-level** – this works on the whole report and filters every visualization and page in the report.

To set the filters, go to Visualizations>Filters and choose which filter you want. Columns can be dragged from a Field in any filter and you click on them to apply the filter. Filters and page and report level work the same way whereas those on a visualization have an extra feature – they can filter metrics or data.

All the filters are saved with the report and will not be shown visually when you look at it. For this reason, always add descriptions to your filters as part of the title of the report, Sales in 2018, for example, rather than just Sales.

Summary

Now you have had a quick look around Power Bi, let's look at what we learned:

- Power Bi provides data analysis tools and a way of getting meaningful insights on your data. It is a cloud service

- For a dashboard to be built, you require a dataset, at least one report, and the dashboard itself. The dataset is the data source; the reports are a way of creating visualizations that may use visual interactions to connect them, while the dashboard is a one-stop place where reports and/or visualizations are kept together

- Natural language queries can be used for creating your visualizations. You can also use full reports or Quick Insights

- Reports can be decorated with pictures, shapes and text boxes

- Visual interactions are not used to connect dashboard visualizations. These interactions will only work on those visualizations in reports but, if required, reports can be pinned as live pages in your dashboard as a way of keeping the capability for interaction intact.

That completes our look at the basics; in Chapter two, we look at the dashboard in more detail.

Chapter 2

Sharing Your Dashboard

In the last chapter, we met Donald, the budgeting manager of Corus. We watched while he created a dashboard, containing his sales analysis. But that really is just the first step for creating his budget. He now needs his colleagues involved so he needs to share what he has already done. Once he has done that, he can collect in the figures and feedback from his managers so that the budget can be completed. And, not only that, but he also has to decide how the reports and the data that come from this are shared with his team members.

In this chapter, we will watch as Donald learns how to achieve his goals by using the Power BI features, among other services.

Inviting Users to See Dashboards

Donald now wants his colleague, Susan, regional manager for Germany, to see the dashboard so he opens it in its Power Bi account and clicks the button that says Share, found in the top-right corner of the dashboard.

A dialog box opens, titled Share Dashboard, and using this, Donald can send an invitation to Susan. Looking closer at this dialog box, we can see that his box has two tabs on it – one to Invite and one entitled Shared With. Both are self-explanatory – in the Invite tab, you type in the email addresses of all the people you want your dashboard shared with. You can even include a message if you like, one that every invitee will see. Looking towards the bottom, you can see a checkbox that says, Allow Recipients to Share Your Dashboard and another checkbox that says, Send Email Notification to Recipients. If you check this second box, Power Bi will send an email to all recipients with a link to the Dashboard.

When you type a name into the box, Power Bi may make suggestions for the email address. This happens when the invitees are co-workers in the same company as you. You can type in the full email address if it doesn't get suggested to you, usually when you are sharing with a person or persons who don't share the domain name that your address has. We'll talk more about this later in this chapter. For now, you can add as many recipients as you want.

If you do not check the Email Notification box, you will then have to click on the Shared With tab and copy the link that leads to your dashboard – you can then send this link to the invitees after clicking the Share button. Every email address provided then gives the individual who owns that address access to the dashboard but they won't get a notification via email.

On the tab called Access, you will see the Dashboard Link box and, in this is the URL that leads to the dashboard. That is the link that you must copy and send to each invitee if you opt not to have a notification sent through Power BI or if you prefer to use your own email address to send the invites. That is a useful option; using your own email address ensures that recipients will recognize it and there is less chance of it being sent to their spam box. Otherwise, they will see one with the sender's address of no-reply@powerbi.com and may just delete it if they don't know what it is. You will also see, under the Access tab, a list of all the users you gave access to your dashboard, along with any privileges assigned to them.

When Susan receives her email, if she has never used Power Bi before, clicking the link in the email to open the dashboard will direct her to the Power BI website. First, she will need to register, the same way that Donald had to when he first started using it. If she is already a registered user, opening the link will take her to the dashboard and she can see everything that Donald can, including all those reports that go with the visualizations Donald pinned onto the dashboard. What she can't do is make any changes to the layout of the dashboard, nor can she change any of the reports. At this stage, the only permission she has is read-only. If Donald wants to let other users make changes to the dashboard he must first create a group workspace and we'll discuss that a bit later in this chapter.

Once Donald has invited Susan, she will be able to open that dashboard in a Power Bi session. Any dashboard that another user has shared will show up on a guest user's Workspace, a separate pane in the window, and beside the name of the dashboard is an icon indicating it is being shared. This also indicates that the dashboard can only be read and not written to. Right now, all Susan can do is interact with the pinned reports and she can open those reports that relate to the visualizations with just a mouse-click on the visualization. She cannot change or modify them in any way. If the reports have not been listed in the Workspace, she can still open them via the dashboard but won't be able to change them because the Edit Report feature is disabled for cases like this.

Inviting External Users

So far, Donald has sent Susan an invite to look at the dashboard. She already works in his organization and her email shares his domain name of @Corus-bi.com. What if Donald wanted to invite someone who works outside of the company?

An explanation is needed here before we can go into any details. Power Bi has been designed in such a way that you can share dashboards with anyone in your organization and anyone who is not. Power Bi identifies organizations in these ways:

1. Each user must have an email address that has the company domain name

2. Power Bi will not accept any generic email domain, such as gmail.com or hotmail.com. Each organization must have a domain name that is unique and every user must have an email that shares that domain name. All users whose email shares that domain name are considered by Power Bi to be a part of the same company.

3. Users who use Microsoft Azure Active Directory and/or Microsoft Office 365 will probably have a different domain name but still belong to that company. This is the only exception to having a different email domain but being in the same company for the purposes of Power Bi.

So, that probably all seems a little bit restrictive at first glance but the reality is that you can share your dashboards with users from different companies and the method you use is exactly the same as sharing within your company. The only difference is, when you type in an email address that has a different email domain, you will get a warning message telling you that the domain is outside your organization.

One important thing you need to understand is the difference between internal and external users:

- **Internal Users** – internal users (those within your company) can be invited to see your dashboard, either by sending them the dashboard URL or an email with a link in it. To get the URL, a user must have authorization; if they don't, they can request permission when they click on the URL.

- **External Users** – external users (those in a different organization) can be invited to see a dashboard but they must receive an email invitation first. Once they get that invitation, they need to sign in to Power BI and they MUST use the email address the invitation was sent to. If this is their first time using Power Bi, they can set up a free account.

Lastly, reports can be published on the web but you cannot publish a dashboard. To publish the report, choose the one you want, click on File and then on Publish to Web. A dialog box will open, entitled Embed In A Public Website (Preview); click the option to Create Embed Code. A public webpage is then created and anybody can go to it. You should bear in mind that you have absolutely no control over who can see this report so, anyone who gets hold of the URL can see it. For this reason, an important one, you should only go down this route when you intend to publish reports that the public should see, for example, one that you add to your own company website.

The feature called Publish to Web will walk you through the process of setting up a public page, of obtaining the URL that can be sent via email or, if you are embedding the report in one of your own websites, the HTML code you need to use.

Creating Group Workspaces

Back to Donald and Susan. After Donald sent Susan an invite, he suddenly realized that he is going to have to do the exact same for every single dashboard that he creates. And, as more people get involved in budgeting, every one of them will need an invitation to see every individual dashboard shared with that group. Fortunately, he finds that Power Bi offers him an easy way; he can create a user group that contains all the users he wants and he can use this to share his dashboards very easily. And he can give some users within the group editing rights too, thus increasing the collaboration level between the users in the group.

There is a caveat to this – you must be in possession of a Power Bi Pro license; this cannot be done on the free version. You do get a free 60-day trial of Power Bi Pro, which gives you a decent amount of time in which to evaluate the features to see if it is a good fit for your organization.

Assuming that Donald has opted to purchase the Pro license, creating a group workspace is quite easy. Go into the My Workspace Pane, which you find underneath the workspace list, and click on the + button, which you will see on the right side of the option to Create a Group. When Donald clicks on this + button, he sees a dialog box, titled Create a Group, open. He calls his group Budget 2019 and, to start with, the group will have Donald as the administrator, with Susan as a group member. Clicking on the Privacy section, Donald sees that he has the option to define the group's privacy levels. He has two settings for the group, the first determining the group visibility – to members only or by other company users who are not yet group members. The choices are:

Public - the group activity can be seen by anyone

Private – only those approved group members can see the activity

The Public setting then specifies the modification of the group members, again with two options:

- Members can edit content

- Members can only have view-only access

If you opt for view-only, the only members who can edit any dashboard in the group are the administrators. Donald sets the group up as Private and provides all members with permission to edit the content so now Susan can both see everything in the group workspace and she can edit the dashboard and the reports. They will also see a list of the group workspaces of which they are members.

With Donald's new group set up, he can now create dashboards and reports in the group and Susan will immediately be able to see them. However, first, the data for the reports muse be imported to the group; it isn't possible to move the reports he created earlier into his personal workspace into the group space. It takes time to import the data and create the reports so, if you know from the start that you are working with a group, create your group workspace right from the outset; it will save you a lot of time and hassle later on.

Enabling Sharing with OneDrive for Business

Before he can go any further, Donald thinks about whether the data sources can be shared, rather than just the dashboards and the reports. Specifically, he wants other colleagues to have the ability to input their data into Excel files, allowing him to create his budget using workbooks that several people will have modified.

Earlier, we saw how Donald had to copy the data from the Excel files he was sent by the regional managers. He then needed to split all the values down into separate months in the table he used to create his report in Power Bi. What he wants is for other users to be able to edit the data in the Excel files so he doesn't have to do it all. To do this, in another worksheet he names Budget, Donald comes up with a Budget table and then copies the Region and Brand values to it.

In the table, he creates a formula that Power Bi will use to allocate the value of the budget across 12 months. Now Donald wants this workbook shared with his colleagues so they can modify the Budget table content directly in a way that the new values will be automatically applied to the dashboards and reports in Power Bi.

The best way of doing this is to use OneDrive for Business. Most people have heard of OneDrive, the personal cloud service for storage. While files can be shared on OneDrive, it is somewhat limited in terms of using it as a source of data for Power Bi. In particular, there are limits in terms of automatically refreshing data. Those limitations are removed by OneDrive for Business and users get far more control. And, with full Office 365 integration, OneDrive for Business offers full support for groups, which makes file and document sharing much easier. To gain access to OneDrive for Business, Donald clicks on the yellow button in the top-left corner of Power Bi (it has nine small squares on it). Then he clicks the tile titled OneDrive and the app webpage opens. Here, Donald can upload his workbook to the group her created called Budget 2019.

When you define a group in Power Bi, it will automatically correspond to an Office 365 group and this gives you a OneDrive for Business folder where documents can be placed for sharing.

When Donald has uploaded his file, it shows up in the files list for the Budget 2019 folder. On the same screen, there is also a Sync button; this is used to obtain information about synchronizing with local computers. This allows you to make changes to the file in a local folder on your PC and then upload updates automatically to the OneDrive shared folder. This results in all the files in the OneDrive folder being available for all group members to see and to use as potential data sources for the Power Bi reports.

Donald has shared the file to Budget 2019 and, later, he will request that all the other members of the group update their own budget data. However, before he does that, he wants a report prepared to show the total (aggregated) of all the budget figures for the regions and that compares the figure with those from previous years.

Back in Power Bi, Donald goes to the available workspaces and chooses Budget 2019. All the reports, dashboards, and the datasets for the group are listed but, to start with, the lists are all empty.

Donald wants to use the data stored in the Excel file, now currently on OneDrive in the group folder, to create a new dashboard and a new report. Doing this requires a similar approach to when he did this for the first time (back in Chapter one). However, rather than uploading a local file from his own PC this time, he clicks on the tile for OneDrive as his source of data. The tile is titled OneDrive – Budget 2019. This is because Donald already uses the workspace for Budget 2019 and that results in the corresponding OneDrive file being cited as a potential data source. As far as Power Bi is concerned, the major difference between OneDrive files and local files is that a local file can't update reports that are based on it automatically whereas the OneDrive file can do this without the need for the user to be involved.

When Donald has chosen the OneDrive – Budget 2019 tile, a window opens asking him to choose which file you want to be connected to Power Bi. As the folder only has one file in it this is the one that Donald clicks, followed by clicking the Connect button. When he has chosen the OneDrive for Business file, Donald has to make a decision on how he wants to use the file.

He has two options for this – he choose to Import Excel Data Into Power Bi or Connect, Manage, And View Excel in Power Bi. You would choose the first option if you want the Excel file used as a source of raw data for reports. Or you could opt to copy an Excel file as it is, using the Power Pivot da model (if you have one) and all features in Excel, like PivotCharts, PivotTables, and any other visualization. If that is what you want, you would choose the second option. Donald opts to use the first choice and he clicks on the Import button.

He now has a dataset called Sales 2018 and Budget 2019. In this dataset, there are two tables, one called Sales and once called Budget2019. This is because, when the Excel file was imported, it had two worksheets in it, each with a table. The Budget2019 table is the one that other manager will modify; they will add in the numbers for their own area budgets. The Sales table remains unchanged from how it was in Chapter one, when Donald made a change to the Budget column by adding in a formula to look for the corresponding value in Budget2019 and allocating it on a month-by-month basis. As such, when a row is updated in Budget2019, the Sales table is updated automatically by Excel.

Donald can now create a report based on his new dataset. He does this by dragging the available fields over to the central pane in the report. What he wants to achieve with the report is to give an overall look at the budget, divided down into Country/Region and Brand. To do this, he opts to use a matrix visualization and, in this, he adds three fields from the Sales table – Brand (rows), Country/Region (columns), and Budget (values). However, he suddenly spots that he has two tables with identical fields; this could cause some confusion. Because the budget is being allocated in the table for Sales, it would be better if the Budget2019 table could be hidden so it didn't show up in the Sales table.

When an Excel file is imported, every table in it will become a part of the data model in Power Bi and will be visible. Later, we'll be looking at how these data models can be controlled but, for now, all Donald wants to do is create a report and he knows that it is best to use the Sales table fields because he will also be able to create a clustered column chart. This will be under the matrix and will show a comparison of the budget with the sales in previous years.

Donald completes his report and saves it, naming it Budget Totals. Both of the visuals are pinned to a brand new dashboard of the same name. Donald has added Susan to the group already so he sends her an email and asks her to review the budget numbers for Germany and make any necessary edits.

When Susan gets the email, she immediately signs into Power Bi and can see the shared dashboard. She clicks on the Budget 2019 workspace and opens OneDrive, where she chooses the Sales 2018 and Budget 2019 file. Now the workbook content loads in her browser and she clicks on the worksheet called Budget. On the menu bar, she clicks on the option to Edit Workbook and then on Edit in Excel Online. She can now edit the file directly in her browser.

She makes changes to the Germany budget for both Corus and A. Datum because she knows that the estimation will be affected by different product lifecycles and market conditions.

To make sure the new values have been allocated properly, she clicks the worksheet called Sales and can see, straightway, that the new value for A. Datum has been allocated and divided down into 12 months, an identical figure for each one. Mentally, she notes that the allocation does not take product seasonality into account so, when she meets with Donald, she will bring this up.

Net, she goes to the Power Bi dashboard for the Budget Totals and sees that the new figure has been represented properly in the matrix, and all other values have been correctly updated to. This pleases her and gives her confidence that Donald will be able to build accurate reports.

Over the course of this chapter, we watched how Donald came up with a collaborative environment, using OneDrive for Business and groups. Collaborations of this nature require Power Bi Pro and OneDrive for Business licenses – don't forget, if you subscribe to Office 365, you will get a subscription to OneDrive for Business automatically.

When you use groups, files can be shared in OneDrive for Business with group members only. If you want to include someone external to the group, the Power Bi personal workspace must be used along with the personal folder from OneDrive.

If you don't have OneDrive for Business, it is possible to use the standard personal OneDrive but things would be a little different. While you can share Excel workbooks in OneDrive and have those you share it with edit it, the workbook can only be imported to the Power Bi personal workspace and not into a group one.

As a recap, you can do this:

- Create Excel workbooks on OneDrive for Business

- Share the file with users, both internal and external to your organization – be aware of the limitations with OneDrive for Business

- Import the file to a Power Bi dataset

- Use it in dashboards and reports. These can be shared only with people in the organization.

A similar thing can be done with standard OneDrive but you lose the benefit of group members getting automatic file visibility that they get with OneDrive for Business.

Using Mobile Devices to View Reports and Dashboards

Any user who has access to Power Bi can see these reports and dashboards, even using a native app on a mobile device. You can get native Power Bi apps for iOS, Android and Windows and these also have extra features, including annotations; these apps also get updates with new features on a regular basis.

So, back to Donald, he could, perhaps, want to show his dashboard to a colleague in a meeting and he wants to use his Windows 10 tablet. The meeting room doesn't have a very good internet connection so he takes full advantage of a neat feature in the mobile app – the offline availability of the dashboard. This feature also lets you view your reports offline, even when there are no interactive capabilities. As such, Donald can see all the data that was available when the report was last refreshed and this provides him with sufficient information for the meeting.

One thing you might spot is that the Power Bi mobile app shows different visuals of the presentations but you do get a nice feature – the ability to zoom in on a visualization and benefit from bigger graphics to navigate your way around. This makes numbers easier to read as well. On an Android smartphone, the visualization is different too, with the visualizations in one vertical column; you also get the ability to zoom in on them individually.

Any user who has a need to input budget data into an Excel file can use the mobile Excel app. The user interface is fully optimized, allowing users a much better experience than the standard web interface for Excel online.

Because there are so many different operating systems, each mobile app may look a little different. The idea here is just to let you know what options are available in terms of tools that work well with Power Bi. Give the applications a go for yourself using your own data and work out what you can and can't display on your mobile device.

Summary

In chapter two we looked at ways of sharing reports, dashboards and raw data with others in the organization:

- Users within your organization can be invited to look at dashboards as well as any reports that underlie it

- If you want anyone outside of the organization to see them, you need to make sure they have an account within the same domain

- Reports may be published on webpages but keep in mind that the report can be seen by anyone. This should not be an option for any sensitive or private data, only for that you public should be able to see

- User groups can be created in the organization and datasets, dashboards, and reports can be shared among the group

- The same groups may be used with OneDrive for Business so that other users may edit data in the shared reports; this data is then updated automatically after any change

- Native applications can be used for reports and dashboards to be displayed on mobile devices

In chapter three, we take a look at data refresh.

Chapter 3

A Look at Data Refresh

Let's go back to Donald. While he gets to grips with Power Bi, he has started to share the dashboards and reports that he created with his regional managers around the world. They all love the fact that they can see these reports on any device and share their ideas while all seeing the exact same data. However, they have concerns. The sales data they are looking at is for October 208 and now they are in the middle of December. The figures they are looking at no longer represent the best data on which sales should be forecast and that is a very important factor in products with a clear seasonality.

As such, Donald needs to get the very latest sales data and use it to refresh his Excel model. With the regional managers urging him on, he does this every single morning until he starts to wonder if there is any way of automating this process. The answer to that is yes; Power Bi does provide a data refresh option.

Introducing Data Refresh

In the first two chapters, we looked at the basic workings of Power Bi – how to upload workbooks with data in them, how to build dashboards and report, and share them with others, both internal and external to the organization. We also mentioned data refresh briefly – how to upload new versions of your workbooks and how to automate things using OneDrive for Business.

For both of these, to update the data Donald had to manually refresh what was in his Excel file and then upload it, using OneDrive for Business or the Power Bi UI, back to Power Bi. As far as data refreshing goes, Power Bi gives you a lot of control but to learn it requires you to pay attention to detail. I would suggest that you read this chapter first and then go back and work through it a bit at a time – there are a few small but incredibly important details that you need to be aware of before you can decide on a strategy for data refreshing.

Perhaps even more importantly, up to this point, I have kept things very simple, showing you just the basics. Now we get more complicated as we delve right into the real details of how to work with Power Bi. From here on, the details are extremely important.

First, let's look at what we really mean by 'refresh'. In context with this chapter, refreshing does not mean that you are manually updating your workbook and saving it as a separate version of the file. Instead, what we want is for the workbook to update automatically and we do that by using a connection that goes to the source database from where the data was originally queried.

Let's look at the four steps Donald has in his system for data processing:

IT retrieves the data from the database and passes it to Donald in an Excel file that has the latest sales figures

Donald then copies the data manually into another version of the workbook for Sales 2018

Next, he saves the file in a way that OneDrive can upload it straight to the cloud

Last, the file content is loaded by Power Bi from OneDrive and Power Bi will update its own data model.

In step three, the Excel file will do an automatic computation of the forecasts the regional managers generate and it does this using one or more formulas. The managers then save the results to OneDrive and they are available in Power Bi straight away.

So far, what Donald has learned about data refresh is useful in making step four into an automated process. Now, he wants the first two steps to be automated but this will need a more in-depth understanding of the internal workings of Power Bi.

The Power Bi Refresh Architecture

Let's look at what goes on when a workbook is uploaded to Power Bi. We'll use the example of the workbook uploaded by Donald to examine the process so, if you recall, there was a table in his workbook.

Donald moves his data from the SQL Server to Excel. He then uploads the excel file to OneDrive and this is where Power Bi reads it. Once it has read the file, Power Bi will generate an SSAS database – a SQL Server Analysis Services. This will use the Power Bi user interface to compute the reports and the dashboards. Complicated? It is but, luckily for you, all the complexity is hidden by Power Bi and that makes it much easier for you to use your Excel files for generating reports. However, if you are going to understand the way that data refresh works, you do need to see the big picture, the entire flow of the information.

In order to make use of data refresh, you need to be able to pull your data from its source – in our case, this is SQL Server. Then you need to be able to push it straight into the SSAS model Power Bi generated. In simple terms, you need a data flow that bypasses both OneDrive and Excel so it flows as you see below:

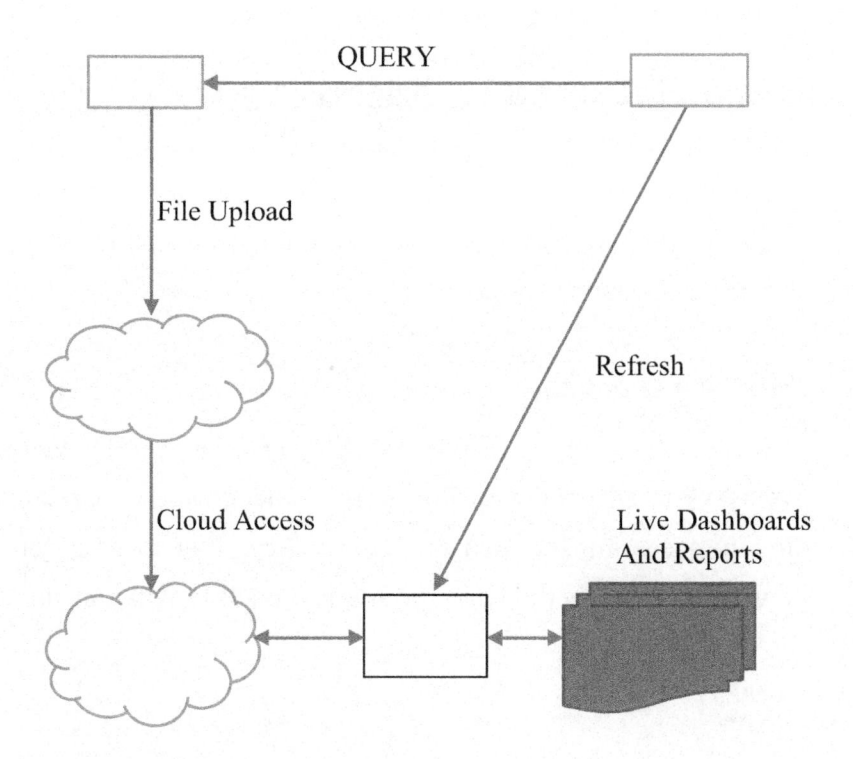

The steps on the left-hand side, highlighted in blue, are the steps we want to be removed. To make that happen, you need to do the following:

You cannot use a plain Excel table for the dataset; Power Bi has got to know how the source database is to be queried so that the data can be refreshed. That means it can't rely on asking either IT or you. Instead, the method has to be formalized and a language that Power Bi understands must be used.

The SSAS engine needs to have a way of accessing that source database. Usually, databases like this are located in the organization or on your own laptop/desktop. As such, you need a piece of software that can implement the connection between the source and Power Bi.

You must be sure that you fully understand these requirements before you continue with this chapter. When you get to the next couple of sections, you will note that I left out much of the technical complexity behind data refresh but it is important that you remember the above scenario.

The Power Bi Desktop

Cast your mind back to chapter one; do you remember that there are two ways to interact with Power Bi – the Power Bi Desktop or directly accessing the web service. We're going to focus on the Power Bi Desktop for now, an application that will run on your computer locally while still providing all the web features and a whole load more besides, including data model options.

By making use of the Desktop, you do not need to use the web service for creating the data model. Instead, Power Bi Desktop gives you all the Power Bi modeling capabilities, at your full disposal.

So, why would you need to use the Desktop if the web service is perfectly able to build your model? Well, there are a number of reasons but we'll focus on just one of them for now – the fact that you can describe your dataset details and this fulfills the first requirement from the refresh scenario we looked at earlier. Before we get that far, the Power Bi Desktop has to be downloaded and installed.

Go to the Power Bi website and look at the right of the menu bar (top of the screen). Click Download and then click on Power Bi Desktop. Once it has downloaded, the Power Bi Desktop wizard will give you instructions on installing it. When you've finished, start the app and you will see a Welcome screen, followed by the Power Bi Desktop window.

You may notice that the Power Bi Desktop UI is very much like power Bi but, as you will find out, Power Bi Desktop can do so much more. It is more complicated than the web service but it does give you the Power Bi engine power at your fingertips.

As you do with Power Bi, you need to give the Desktop some data. Because the data is in an Excel file, you can use to start practicing. Go to the Data group and click on Get Data in the ribbon; click Excel and a dialog box opens. Choose the file you want and click on Open.

Another dialog box, titled Navigator, opens, where you choose the source file. When you choose Excel as your data source, you can decide whether to load from worksheets or tables. We're going to work with our table – be aware that you could have tables and worksheets with the exact same name; an icon beside them is the only thing that will differentiate them.

Choose the Sales table and click on Load; this imports the table in and you can shut the dialog box down. Things should start to look a little familiar now and, using the Visualization and Fields panes, you can start building reports in Desktop in the exact same way as you did in the web service earlier. The biggest difference is that, rather than cloud interaction, the work is all on your PC.

As you build the report, you will start to see just how friendly the Power Bi Desktop is to use, offering neat features such as Copy and Paste. So if, for example, you wanted a visualization like the one you created earlier, you simply copy it and then paste it. There is more to the Desktop than this but it is the little features that make things much easier for you.

Publish to Power Bi

Back to the exercise we started earlier; when your model has been built, save it and call it Sales PBD. Right now, the report is on your PC as a local file and it can only be viewed by you. However, your ultimate goal here is to get your model published over the cloud service Power Bi uses, just so you can use all the Power Bi features, including sharing and the ability to view it on a mobile device.

Go up to the ribbon at the top in Power Bi Desktop and click on the Home tab. Then go to Share and click on Publish. You will now be asked to sign in to Power Bi and you might be asked if you want to make any modifications to your changes. As I said earlier Power Bi Desktop runs on your PC locally and it doesn't need a Power Bi account – until you want to publish. If, at this point, you don't have an account you will be asked to create one. Once you have signed in, the publish operation is confirmed and you get a link to your published report.

Click on the link to open it in the Power Bi website and you see a dataset. It has a name of Sales PBD, the name you gave it earlier, and there is also a report called the same. With Power Bi Desktop, you can create models and reports and, when you publish to Power BI, both are created.

Once you have gotten used to this, you will find that it is one of the most convenient ways of developing reports. When you work with Power Bi Desktop, you will find it far more productive; there isn't any need to be connected to the internet and you get all the power offered by window applications. When you are done you publish the model and this overwrites any other version you may have created previously.

As a recap:

Power Bi Desktop is a locally run Windows application that provides you all the features you get with the cloud service

Models can be built using Power bi Desktop and you can save them straight to your desktop

Power Bi Desktop models can be published to Power Bi but you must have a valid Power Bi account first.

As we were meant to be discussing data refresh, how on earth is all this relevant? Where does Power Bi Desktop fit in? It's simple – files created in Power Bi Desktop have all the information that is required for refreshing the model. What we did in our file was created a link from the Excel file that had all the budget figures and the model built in Power Bi Desktop.

In the first chapter, when our file was first uploaded to Power Bi, all we did was copy it. With the Power Bi Desktop, you can create a link between the files by writing queries. In all truthfulness, we don't actually write them; Power Bi Desktop does it all for us.

There is just one thing missing now – a way that Power Bi can access our Excel file, our data source. Because the original file is on a local PC, it cannot be accessed by Power Bi cloud and so, in the next section, we'll look at how to solve this.

How to Install the Power Bi Personal Gateway

Here, we introduce you to a piece of software called the Power Bi Personal Gateway. This is able to form a connection with the Power Bi cloud service and enable the queries in the Power Bi Desktop file to be carried out. Download it from the official Power Bi website but, after clicking Download, click on Power Bi Gateways instead. You will then be asked to make a choice between these two options:

Personal Gateway – for use with your personal datasets; simple to install but the features for security and monitoring for multiple users are limited.

Enterprise Gateway – offers a lot more functionality but is more complex to set up and use; you will likely need the involvement of your IT department.

Let's pop back and see how Donald is getting on.

He is still having a play about with Power Bi, experimenting to see what it can do so, right now, he has no interest in complex systems. Instead, he opts for the Personal Gateway. Before he sets it up, he needs to know how it is implemented.

If he decides to set it up using administrator privileges, it runs as a service. Alternatively, he could install as just a standard user and this will mean it running as any normal program does. So, where is the difference? When it runs as a service, it will continue running even if there aren't any users signed into the PC. If it runs as a normal program, it can only run if Donald is signed in. This could be quite relevant when he decides that his data needs to be refreshed while he is at home, working on the Power Bi service while his business laptop has been left at work; it is switched on but no-one is logged in. In a case like this, where it runs as a service, the refresh would be successful; if it runs as a normal program, it won't be.

The choice is really down to you but Donald is going to run his personal gateway as an administrator. One the gateway is installed, it must be started so configuration can be completed. In fact, it will need your Power Bi credentials so it can access Power Bi – it has to get in touch with the cloud service and start answering the queries the service sends.

Once Donald has successfully signed in, he will see a Power Bi Gateway Personal dialog box. Here, he needs to input more credentials – his Windows credentials. These are needed because Donald has opted to run the gateway as a service, which, if you remember, will run even when there isn't anyone signed in. These credentials are needed to gain access to connections and files on the PC. In simple terms, the gateway has the same access rights as Donald does on his PC, allowing it to access data sets and files just as if it were Donald accessing them.

When it's all done, the gateway will tell you that there is one operation that still needs to be done. You need to go to powerbi.com and complete the data source setup. There, you will need to reinput your credentials.

Donald has almost finished configuring his gateway; his final step is to go to the Power Bi cloud service and click the Configuration button on the menu. He then clicks on Settings and a new page opens; here, he can configure his settings for each individual data set.

He sees an alert on the Settings page and it has two pieces of very important information:

It tells you that the gateway is connected online and is running on a PC with his name.

The data set isn't ready just yet and, even if the gateway setup were complete, you would still need to provide specific credentials for the data source.

Why is it necessary to do this for each data source? Because, simply, each data source may need to have different credentials. The Sales PDB file Donald created is stored on his local computer so, because he provided his Windows credentials, it can be accessed automatically. In that case, when he clicks the Edit Credentials option, he needs to provide an authentication method. His only option is the Windows authentication method so Donald clicks on the Sign In option and doesn't need to input his credentials again.

However, other data sources that don't use Windows authentication will require you to provide usernames and passwords so the gateway can make the connection to the data source when the refresh operation is done.

Automatic Refresh Configuration

Once all your credentials are set up, you can refresh the data source. You have new provided Power Bi with everything it needs to do this, be it on-demand or on a schedule. If you click on the Schedule Refresh option and expand it, you get the option of defining when an attempt should be made to refresh the dataset. Should the refresh fail, you also get an option of being alerted by email so you can take any necessary action.

At this point you have two choices – wait until the refresh has happened or, just to make sure it is all properly set up, you can force it. To do this, go to the Dataset section and look in the left navigation pane – you should see an ellipsis on the right side of the data source; click on this. Next, click on Refresh now.

When you request a refresh, Power Bi will prepare it and start. Depending on how large the dataset is and how fast your internet connection is, this can take anywhere from a few seconds up to a good deal longer. To see when a dataset was refreshed last, go back to the window where you requested the refresh and you can see when it happened.

Summary

Here, we learned about data refresh:

- Simple data models based on Excel files can be uploaded to Power Bi and, using a Personal Gateway, they can be refreshed. A Personal Gateway enables Power Bi to have access to your local datasets

- Power Bi Desktop is required when you want to run data refresh on models that are more complex, such as the SQL Server models

- Power Bi Desktop enables you to create models that have the required information to allow a connection between the cloud service and Personal Gateway so the dataset can be retrieved.

If you have a free Power Bi license your data can be refreshed daily; if you need several refreshes per day, you will need a Pro license.

In the next chapter, we will look deeper into the Power Bi Desktop.

Chapter 4

Using Power BI Desktop

In the previous chapter, we started to talk about data refresh. Donald, the budgeting manager for Corus, learned how to refresh Power Bi models based on Excel workbooks with the last three years' sales data and a forecast for the following year. To do that, he needed to learn how to use Power Bi Desktop, a windows app that provides all of Power Bi's modeling power to your desktop.

Now Donald needs to move on and learn more about building his model. Up to now, the solution he has come up with is dependent on the last three years' sales figures being provided by IT. Thankfully, Donald has found out that the figures can be loaded directly from the company's data warehouse using Microsoft SQL Server. Now, whenever a data refresh is done by Power Bi, the latest data is automatically retrieved, resulting in the entire model being updated.

Here's what Donald needs to do:

- Load the sales data directly from the warehouse rather than the Excel file. To do this, he needs access to the corporate database but he can get access to whatever data is required from the IT department

- Load the forecasts for the following year from the file updated daily by the region/country managers.

The Power Bi Desktop provides everything that Donald needs so let's explore it a bit deeper and see how we can use this powerful application.

Connecting To a Database

Donald is already aware of how to load the data from Excel into the Power Bi Desktop; he did it by using the Excel file provided by IT. This time, it is a database he needs to work from and, to access it, he can get the correct credentials from IT, allowing him to query the database and find what information he requires. The Corus database administrator, Kathy, gives Donald read-only access to a view that will show him the exact same dataset that she sends to him daily.

By doing this Kathy is happy because she won't have to complete the Excel workbook now. If Donald can load all the data and get his insights himself, her workload will lighten, leaving her free to concentrate on more pressing matters. As such, she tells Donald that he has access to look at Sales2018 on the CorusDBServer, using his Windows credentials for access. He can only read it, not edit it so there is no chance if him causing any problems. Because of the level of database security, there is a safeguard in place that nothing can happen to it.

Opening Power Bi Desktop, Donald goes to the Home tab and clicks on Get Data. This time, though, he chooses the option for SQL Server. A dialog box opens, he inputs the connection information provided to him by Kathy and then clicks on OK.

Power Bi Desktop will now make the connection to the database and will show Donald a list of available data tables. In that list is the Sales2018 file created by Kathy and Donald clicks it so Power Bi displays a preview of what's in it. Once Donald has made his choice, he clicks Load. Power Bi Desktop will now ask him what interaction method he wants to use so he clicks the Import option and then on Ok.

Let's step back for a minute and learn a bit more about the connection option. It is important and it will give you a better understanding of the way connections work in Power Bi.

When you opt for the Import option, Power Bi will make a connection to the database. Then it will load the information and store it inside the Power Bi data model. Then you can do what you need to do with your data in Power Bi desktop without needing a connection to the database. The only time you need a connection is when you need the data refreshed.

The Power Bi Desktop doesn't load any data into its own internal database; instead, it uses DirectQuery to run queries back to the original database whenever it needs a chart drawn or a query run. As such, there is a permanent connection between the database and the Power Bi Desktop.

The contrast between the timings of the queries is reflective of one key difference – when you choose Import, you work only with data that is as up to date as the last data refresh but, with DirectQuery, you will always have the very latest information when you want to create a report.

At first look, it would seem then, that using DirectQuery is the best method for loading the data but this isn't strictly true. If your data is refreshed on a regular basis, it is likely that, while you will see one set of figures when you look at a report, within minutes, even seconds that data could be completely different. This is incredibly frustrating when you are attempting to analyze a year's worth of data, like Donald is. And numbers that are constantly changing can be quite disturbing. There is also the fact that, while real-time data can be useful at times, it does come with a cost – the query speed. By its nature, DirectQuery is a good deal slower than when you work with data already on your device, data that you can access directly via the Power Bi Desktop.

Lastly for this section, it is worth bearing in mind that, while DirectQuery works perfectly well with Power Bi for Desktop on your computer, when it comes to publishing the model to Power Bi, a method of communication is required by the cloud service to the internal database server. This is done through the Enterprise

Gateway, the more advanced Gateway version we mentioned in chapter three.

Donald is trying to analyze the data for an entire year so he doesn't have a need for the data to be frequently updated. As such, he opts for Import and the data loading takes just a few seconds. He spots that the table's full name is far too long by he can rename it by right-clicking it and then on Rename in the popup menu.

Once the table has been given a new name, there doesn't look to be any difference between this and the previous models created by Excel data. However, there is a big difference – the Power Bi model has now been linked to the SQL Server database, which is the original data source. When the data is refreshed by Power Bi Desktop, it doesn't require the Excel file. Instead, it directly connects to the database, which means it always has up to date information rather than relying on manually updated information. What Donald has done is removed the middle step – Excel – thus saving a significant amount of time and effort that would have been needed to prepare the file.

Loading Data from Multiple Sources

While it felt great to be working with a database directly. When Donald investigated further, he got a bit of an unpleasant shock. When he used Excel, he could integrate the sales data from the SQL Server and the budget forecast from the Excel file into one table. However, there is no way for the SQL Server database to provide the Excel database because the updates are made by the managers straight to the Excel file.

Solving this will require an even deeper look into how the Power Bi Desktop model is structured internally. In the last chapter, we said that models built in Power Bi Desktop have an internal query that Power Bi Desktop creates for each of the datasets. If basic operations, such as data loading from the SQL Server database or an Excel file, then the internal query is invisible but it is still there and, if needed, you can modify it.

The Power Bi Desktop query language is used by Query Editor and to discuss that language would, in all honesty, run to a few hundred pages. I don't have that much space in this book so, instead, I want to show you some of the more basic Query Editor features so that you can gain a better understanding of what it can do.

Modifying a Query Editor script is easy enough – open the Power Bi Desktop and click the Home tab and then Edit Queries. A new window opens with Query Editor in it and there are several options. At the top is a ribbon with four separate tabs – Home, Transform, Add Column and View. Underneath this is the Query pane, to the left, showing a list of the queries for the specified model. The pane in the middle shows the query result and, on the right is the Query Settings pane, showing the query's properties.

For Donald, as he is already looking at the 2018 data stored on the Corus database, he now wants a new query created to retrieve the information from the Excel file for the budget forecast.

If he wanted to load some data from a new dataset, you would go to the Home tab, click on the New Query group, then on New Source and specify the data you wanted loaded, in this case from the Budget table. Two tables will appear in the Queries pane in the Query Editor window.

Once you are done with your edits, click the Home tab again, click on Close & Apply and the data will be loaded into the Power Bi Desktop. The Fields pane in Desktop will then show the two data sources – the SQL Server database and the Excel table.

How to Use Query Editor

Right now, Donald is at the point where he can create a report that has the tables for Budget and for Sales 2018 in it, sliced by the column for Brand. But there is a nasty shock in store for him – the budget value is identical in every column.

This is somewhat confusing; Donald used the attributes for Brand and Sales2018 from the Sales2018 table and he used the Budget 2019 column from the table called Budget. That doesn't stop the values always being the same and, if that weren't enough, the value always looks to be too high for the brands.

The problem is this – when Donald uses the Sales2018 Brand column, although it has an identical name it is NOT the same thing as taking the values from the Budget table's Brand column. While both columns share a name and values, they aren't the same columns. In fact, if you tried to replace Brand with the Budget table's Brand column, you would get a result much the same but the opposite – the values for the budget are sliced correctly but those for Sales aren't.

Now would be a good time to step aside and look as what the right data model is for Donald to represent his dataset. But I'm not going to do that because it isn't really relevant to this book. What is important is that numbers that come from two tables cannot be sliced using the columns from one of those tables. The only time you can do this is if there is a relationship between the tables.

In order to fix this, the Budget 2019 column needs to be brought into the Sales2018 table (its position in the original file) from the Excel budget table. To be technical about it, we 'join' the tables together, and copy the Budget column for the specified brand and country/region. As it turns out, Query Editor is the ideal tool to do this with.

Query Editor makes it easy to load tables but there is another option – you can modify the auto generated query so it behaves in a different way. Let's go back to Donald and see how it's done.

He goes to the Query Editor window in Power Bi Desktop and he makes a modification to the query for Sales 2018. To do this he chooses the query and then clicks the Home tab on the ribbon. Then he clicks on Merge Queries and the Merge dialog box opens. Here, Donald needs to state which table is the destination and which columns he wants used to join the source and the destination table together. Donald uses the country/region and brand in both of the tables.

When you choose which columns you want to merge, you might see a Query Editor Dialog box that requests you to specify the data source privacy level. These levels are there to make sure that you don't send private data to sources that are external to your own secure area. If you set the wrong level, you could let untrusted sources see sensitive data or you could affect the way the query performs. Donald sets both of his sources to Private because both of them are inside his own network. If you choose to load data from the internet, the source should be marked as Public to ensure information is not sent to the web from a private source.

There is one more option in the Merge dialog box – Join Kind. This is used when you want to choose what will happen to the rows in a table where there are no corresponding rows in the second table. For example, if you have sales for Country/Region but no budget, should you include the sales in the dataset? Normally, the default type of join is used – this is known as a Left Outer join and this will include every row that is in the source table and just those that match it from the other table. For Donald, all the sales are retrieved, along with the budget data for brands and countries/region with sales.

Once Donald has clicked on OK, there will be a new column in the table, it's called NewColumn and the content comes from a table. When two tables are merged, the result will be the original column and a new one that has the Table type. In the new column are all of the rows that relate to the current row from the first table. Donald's table has just one row – where a join is more complex, there could be multiple.

Donald doesn't want the entire table; all he wants is the Budget column so he expands the NewColumn table so that it includes just those columns that he requires. To do this, he clicks on the two arrows next to the name of the column and the Expand Column dialog box opens.

Donald chooses the Budget 2019 column only and this results in that column being available for each of the Sales table rows.

He is nearly finished. The final step is that the column will show the entire budget for the year and the Sales table will contain just the monthly budget. In his Excel file, Donald split the budget value down into 12 equal figures and the same has been done here. To do that, he goes to the Add Column tab and clicks on Add Custom Column under General. This creates a new column that has the Budget 2019 value divided into 12. For the column to be created, Donald has to provide the right expression to compute it. He does that in the Add Custom Column dialog box.

Next, he right-clicks on the Budget 2019 column and removes it because he doesn't need it anymore. Before he saves the query, he needs to define the column's data type. Custom columns are, by default, of the type Any Data that means there is no data type defined. Because Donald needs to aggregate the values, he needs the data type to be Decimal Number.

When he's finished, he has a Sales2018 table that looks exactly the same as its counterpart in Excel. There is one difference – in the new table, the SQL Server database is used to compute the sales values and, on refreshing the model, the latest figures will be retrieved automatically.

Removing or Hiding Tables

This model has one more small problem with it. When Donald used Query Editor, the budget figures were moved into the Sales2018 table, thus creating one table that has all the columns he needs to create his report. But, in the Fields pane, all he can see is the Budget table. This could be confusing for other group members who look at the report.

This can be solved by hiding the Budget table from Fields or by not loading it at all. To hide the table, go to the Fields pane and right-click on the name. A menu appears, click on Hide.

Hidden tables can no longer be seen in the Fields pane but, if you want it to be visible again, simply go to the Context menu on any of the tables in the field pane and click on View Hidden. To make visible again, simply clear the Hide mar beside those you want to see. Hiding tables doesn't make them secure; it is only marked as invisible but it can be seen by any user who uses the interface. Hiding it just keeps the model simple for browsing and less prone to errors.

Donald has decided that he doesn't want the table on there at all; everything he needs for his report is in the Sales 2018 table. Query Editor uses the Budget table to merge the divided budget into Sales 2018 and one this has been done, the Budget table is no longer needed.

An easy way to stop a table being loaded is to go to the Queries pane in Query Editor and right-click the Budget query that is no longer needed. On the menu, remove the checkmark next to Enable Load. You will get a warning message telling you of possible data loss; if you carry on, the table is moved out of the model and the model transforms back to a single-table model and sales 2018 has all the information needed.

Seasonality and Sorting Months

Do you remember, back in chapter two, that Susan was concerned about seasonality? Donald splits his budget figures into 12 equal values but many of the brands have some kind of seasonal effect that has not been considered when the budget is drawn up. And, because some of the brands don't show any sales at all for some months, the report is missing a few months too.

Let's assume that we have the budget report for Wide World Importers, based in China. Donald spots two main issues:

There are no sales figures for either December or January because no sales were made. The rows that correspond to those months are missing and this is a problem. The total budget, as you know has been computed to be divided into 12 equal figures but there are only 10 rows in the total budget figure. That means the values are wrong.

While Donald looks for the missing months, he also spots that the months are not in sequential order, Power Bi, by default, sorts individual columns alphabetically and, as we all know, this isn't the right way to sort months.

Donald wants to solve these problems, starting with the latter because that is the easiest one. To get the months into sequential order, Donald needs to add a new column in his sales table with the numbers from 1 to 12 in it. Right now, this column doesn't exist and there is no functionality predefined that can help him to do it.

If he still had his data in Excel, Donald could manually add the column but the data source is now the SQL Server, from the Corus database. Donald is not able to edit the SQL Server view to do this. Fortunately, Power Bi Desktop makes it simple – when you want to add data to a model, all you do is enter it. Go to Query Editor and click the Home tab on the ribbon. Click New Query and then Enter Data; in the Create Table dialog box, you will see a grid and you can add in any new data to your model. Donald adds two new columns; one containing the months in alphabetical order and the other, the numbers from 1 to 12, starting with January and going through to December.

He saves his data and gives the table a new name of Month Numbers so his next step is to add the Month Number column into his Sales 2018 report. This is similar to something we already did – Donald joins the Sales 2018 table to Month Numbers. This, time there is a relationship based on the names of the months; In the Merge dialog box, check all is as it should be and click on OK.

Once the data is merged, the Month Number column needs to be expanded and the content loaded into the data model in Power Bi Desktop. Now the new column is in the table, you need to tell Power Bi that the month names must be sorted by month number. Go to the Fields pane and click on the month name. On the ribbon, you will see a new tab called Modeling. Click it and then click on Sort By Column, choosing Month Number. The report will now change and the months will be in the correct order.

Now the months are displayed in the right order, Donald can easily see that December and January are not there so he needs to fix it. This is going to take a little work so he needs to do a bit of work beforehand.

First, he has to determine which year is best for determining product seasonality. Looking at his report for Wide World Importers, the yearly sales figures show that there were sales in January 2016 but none in January 2017, so which one does he use to determine January's allocation? He opts for 2017 because it gives him the best figures – you may make different decisions based on your own data but, as I said to you, this is not about budgeting; this guide is all about showing you how Power Bi works.

Once his decision is made, Donald now needs a table that has the number of months where sales occurred in 2017 for each brand and country/region. This is going to take a few steps using Query Editor:

Beginning with Sales 2017, he removes all the columns he doesn't need, keeping just CountryRegion, Brand, Month, Sales2017

All the empty rows in Sales 2017 are removed

The Sales2017 column is removed

He counts the number of months for each brand

The first bit is quite easy. He right-clicks on Sales 2017 in Query Editor and clicks duplicate on the popup menu. This makes a copy of the table, which he names Months Count. Now, in Query Editor, Donald goes to Applied Steps and locates the Delete icon beside each step and removes every step except the first two, which are Source and Navigation. This ensures he returns to the original query. As he is working on a duplicate of the Sales 2017 table, he can do whatever he wants to it because the original one will not be touched.

Now he can delete the columns for Sales2015 and Sales2016 because he doesn't need them right now. He right-clicks on the header of each column and chooses Remove Columns from the popup menu.

Onto step two, Donald spots that the first row in the table has a null value for Sales2017. Right-clicking on the value opens a menu where he clicks on Number Filters followed by Does Not Equal – this means he wants only the rows where Sales2017 is not null to be filtered.

By the time he gets to step three, the Sales2017 column is not relevant anymore so, with a simple right-click on it, Donald can remove it.

Lastly, with step four, a common operation for any dataset, Query Editor provides the functionality Donald needs. First he needs to select the columns that are being grouped by highlighting them and then clicking Group By on the ribbon. In the dialog box that opens, Donald checks that the columns to group and operations for other columns are correct and then clicks on OK and the dataset loads.

This new dataset shows the number of months where figures are available for each brand and for country/region. This is the number to use in the division formula, not 12, so that the correct value is shown for each month. Donald doesn't want this table in his model so, as you saw earlier, he disables loading for it. It is just a helper table and it is used with Sales 2017 using a join operation. The information in it is only useful for the join operation, nothing else.

So, the final step in modifying Sales 2017 uses this figure again but there doesn't need to be any extra steps in your existing query. What you do need to do is replace some of the steps and this requires some thought.

Go to Query Editor and open the query for Sales 2017 again. Start going through the pane for Applied Steps and you will see that what is in the results pane is a reflection of the query once a selected step has been applied. So, for example, if you clicked on Added Custom Step, you would see the Budget 2019 column but this is going to be removed with the next step.

Before that Added Custom Step, a few more steps need to be included and then the budget calculation needs to be modified. Whenever you select an operation from the toolbar, the step is included directly after the one you currently selected. As such, the fourth step of Expanded NewColumn is selected and a new step of merging Months Count and Sales 2017 is added, with the relationship based on Brand and CountryRegion.

Once the column has been added, a different expression is required in the Budget 2019 column. That column needs to be computed to divide the total budget figure by the number of months, just the months where there were sales in 2017. To do this, go to the Applied Steps pane. Next to Added Custom step is a gear icon; this is the settings button – click on it. Change the expression so it reads the correct figure and, when you click on OK, the report will be updated to show the right figures.

Summary

That completes chapter four where you learned about the Power Bi Desktop basics. We will go into more details in the remaining chapters in the book but these are the relevant features:

- Data can be loaded from any database in Power Bi Desktop; SQL Server database was our example

- You can also load from more than one source; we combined SQL server database data with data from Excel

- Query Editor is used to load the data in Power Bi Desktop. It is a powerful feature and we focused on the power it has to merger queries and to add calculations to a query

- We also learned that, while some queries should and can be loaded to the model, others are only of use in value computations for the main queries. As such, those that you do not want in the model should be marked as 'do not load'; this way, they only get used in the Query Editor

- Power Bi Desktop models can be uploaded to Power Bi Online, retaining all the refresh features. When you use the Personal Gateway, a model can be refreshed in the cloud, giving it access to your PC's data

This might look complicated at first sight but, once you get used to doing it, you will find that Query Editor provides a powerful way to help build models.

In chapter five, we turn our attention to retrieving data from services and content packs.

Chapter 5

Retrieving Data from Services and Content Packs

Donald is quietly working away on the 2019 budget when it suddenly comes to him that it might be a useful exercise to look at the stats for all the company website pages that were visited. He could use these insights to try and predict the products that will prove popular in future months.

Power Bi provides lots of content packs and connections so Donald will easily be able to get the data that is generated from cloud services. Plus, the content packs are a useful way of deploying predefined reports and models and sharing them within the organization.

In this chapter, we will watch as Donald learns how to import data into Power Bi from Google Analytics, using a number of techniques. You can also use these techniques to get your data from many different web services.

Consuming Service Content Packs

Donald wants to look at the data relating to website visits by customers, hoping to gain some early insights on potential growth in specific countries/regions. If he sees an increase in visitor numbers in certain areas, he may also see a corresponding growth in sales for that area. If he looks at this data for the previous two years, it could provide him with data that could help with defining the sales targets for each of the countries/regions. This comparison is a very important step in the data analysis that he wants to achieve.

He knows that Google Analytics monitors the company website but he isn't sure if it is supported by Power Bi. Scanning through the documentation for Power Bi, he gets his answer – yes, Google Analytics is supported. The Power Bi service provides a service content pack and also a connector so Donald can start to use this service.

Starting Power Bi, he clicks on the Get button in the bottom-left of the window, and the Get Data page opens. When you ask to get your data from a service, Power Bi will automatically create a data source, a dashboard, and a report that are all connected to the specified service. It used a series of predefined templates to do this and, if you want, these can be modified later. Power Bi uses your login credentials to gain access to the service so the report will always represent your own data.

Donald wants to make use of a content pack so, on the Get Data page he goes to the Content Pack Library section and goes to the Services tile. There, he clicks on Get and a list of available services loads. He finds and clicks Google Analytics and a message opens, providing him with a service description.

He clicks the Connect button and is then asked to pick which authentication method he wants to use for the connection. He only has one option available, which is 0Auth2, so he clicks on Sign In. If you have not previously accessed the service you will need to sign in to the Google Analytics service.

When Donald has signed in, he needs to provide the Power Bi application with offline access. To give Power Bi the authorization necessary to get data for him from Google Analytics, he clicks on the Allow button.

The Connect to Google Analytics dialog box then goes to another page, giving Donald the option of choosing which Google Analytics data he wants in the content pack. He has three options to complete:

Account – the Google Analytics account name – choose from the drop-down list of available names. One user may have access to several accounts.

Property – the property name (a Google Analytics concept) from the data the chosen account owns

View – the view name in the property. Most of the time, the view and the property correspond to one another, unless there are several websites for one account.

Donald completes the options, choosing SQLBI as the Account, DAX Formatter as the Property and the same for View. Then he clicks the Import button and the content library is copied to the selected workspace by the Power Bi service. The connection is then updated using the previously provided information. Lastly, the workspace is populated with the data from Google Analytics and the result is a dashboard, a report, and a dataset with the name of Google Analytics. Donald can rename this if he wants – advisable if you are importing several copies of one content pack into the same space.

In the Google Analytics dashboard, Donald can see information about how much traffic the website received in the previous 30 days. Let's just look at this dashboard for a minute. If you click a visualization, you are taken to a corresponding report showing the data underlying the visualization. All the dashboard visualizations are in the same report, which contains pages filtering the past 30 days' data, such as Total Users, from 90 days, including Site Traffic, or even 180 days, with filters such as Top Pages, Page Performance and System Usage.

Donald can now make changes to the report given him by the content pack or he can make a new report using the existing one and based on the Goggle Analytics dataset. For both of these, one problem arises – this dataset doesn't give Donald all the slicers and measures that are available from the Google Analytics server. Plus, the historical depth doesn't go any further back than 180 days. Why is this?

The engineers responsible for creating the content pack wanted to provide the minimum amount of data to make the reports, keeping the Power Bi file that results from it to a minimum. This leads to an improvement n the way some of the related operations perform. However, there may not be enough information to do what you want to do.

This service pack has provided a useful basic overview of the available data but it isn't enough for Donald. He needs more historical depth if he is going to do trend analysis and the 180-day limit is not enough. Second, he wants one report that shows what the relationship is between the Google Analytics data and other data, such as forecast and past sales. To do this, he needs one dataset that has several connections so it isn't very useful to use the Google Analytics service pack because data models created from datasets copied from content packs cannot be modified; the dashboard and the reports from the content pack can be customized.

What Donald needs to do is create another dataset only using the Google Analytics connection in Power Bi Desktop; no reliance on the content pack.

Creating Custom Datasets from Services

Donald wants some Google Analytics measures shown in the same report, namely those that relate only to the USA, Germany, and China because these are the countries/regions he wants from the budget report. He wants more information than he can get with the content pack on Power Bi too.

Rather than using the read-only, predefined content pack, Donald uses the Power Bi Desktop to form a connection to Google

Analytics and then includes the Google dataset in his budget model. This takes a few steps to complete but it does give him more flexibility in the measures, new tables, calculations, and relationships in his data model.

So, starting with the model he created in the Power Bi Desktop in chapter four, (it has a single table with sales and budget figures in separate columns). This table is useful for analyzing historical sales trends but he also needs other Google Analytics tables; for this, he will need a special connector to import the Google Analytics data straight to the model in Power Bi Desktop.

He starts up Power Bi Desktop and clicks the Home tab on the ribbon. Then he clicks on Get Data followed by More. The Get Data dialog box opens so he clicks Other in the left pane. In the right pane, he clicks on Google Analytics, then Connect.

Now he must sign in to Google to give Power Bi Desktop access to his Google Analytics information. When he has done this, he must choose the measures and the attributes he wants to be imported into the model. In the Navigator dialog box, he sees a list containing all the services that his Google account monitors. Once he has selected the service, he sees a list of all the folders that have the measures and attributes he can choose to import form. Attributes are information that Google Analytics collects, such as geographic and demographic information about website visitors, date-related columns, and lots more that can be used for filtering data. Measures are bits of numeric data that show the size or frequency of an event, such as how many users, how many visits, average page-loading time, and more.

Back to the Home tab in the Power Bi Desktop, Donald chooses Edit Queries and the Query Editor window opens. In the Query Editor he must apply a filter because he only wants limited countries/regions. He clicks on the Country/Region column and chooses the United States, Germany, and China to restrict the data.

Once Donald has confirmed what he wants to be imported, the Power Bi Desktop will send the query onto Google Analytics and the result is imported into a new table. Donald is looking for a key metric of the growth experienced in 2017 of new users. Google Analytics content pack didn't have sufficient historical depth for what Donald needed because he needed data for 2016 and 2017. When you import the data via Power Bi Desktop, there are no limitations so he can get the historical depth he needs. However, to calculate the percentage of the growth, Donald needs to learn the computer language Power Bi uses, DAX.

DAX or Data Analysis Expressions, first appeared in Power Pivot for Excel 2010 and it is based on the formula language in Excel. If you are experienced in using Excel, you should find that a lot of the DAX functions share names and syntax with those in spreadsheets. There are new functions and concepts as well but they do not fall into the scope of this book. In a later chapter, we will be looking briefly at DAX measures though.

Donald is already experienced in using Power Pivot for Excel so he knows how to write his measure. On the Home tab, he clicks on New Measure and adds this measure into the formula bar:

```
New Users Growth =
 IF (
    HASONEVALUE ( Website[Year] ),
    DIVIDE (
       SUM ( Website[New Users] ),
       CALCULATE (
          SUM ( Website[New Users] ),
          Website[Year] = VALUES ( Website[Year] ) - 1
       )
    )
 )
```

Next, the measure is displayed as a new visualization under the metric for New Users, grouped by year, and country/region.

Now Donald has all he needs from Google Analytics and he can put it all in one single report, added to the data that he gets from other sources. We looked at how to load from other data sources in chapter four and, in chapter 6, we will look at how to use DAX to combine it all in one model.

Donald is now ready to publish hos Power Bi Desktop report using Power Bi. He will be able to pin his report to a dashboard giving him one dashboard and one report that was published on Power Bi, based on a customized dataset he used Power Bi Desktop to create, to gain specific data from Google Analytics.

Creating Content Packs for Organizations

Now that Donald has finished creating his Power Bi Desktop report, he wants to be able to share it with his colleagues. What is the best Power Bi tool to help him do this?

He quickly realizes that his report is a decent starting point for even deeper insights his colleagues create and, with the Share feature, he can share just the dashboard and the reports that underlie it. However, he also wants his Google Analytics-based report published as a template his colleagues can use for their reports. The sharing options we have explored up to now are not sufficient for Donald's needs; he needs his colleagues to have the capability to customize those reports and produce new ones that are based on his. Simply sharing the dashboard does not provide this capability and, if he used the group workspace, there would only be one copy of the dashboards and reports for all users. These would not be visible to any user external to the organization but Donald wants his new report to be shared both internally and external to the Budget group.

One solution is a content pack for organizations. This can have reports, datasets, and dashboards in it and any user that gets a copy of it will find that, should a new version of the pack be published their copy would be synchronized automatically. If an object in the pack is customized by a user, it is done on their copy, which will not be synced to the original.

Creating a content pack is easy enough; in Power Bi, click on Settings in the top right corner and then click on Create Content Pack. The dialog box opens and Donald can provide the pertinent information about the pack. He can decide who it should be visible to – anyone in the organization or those in specified groups – and Donald opts for My Entire Organization. He calls the content pack Sales and Website 2017 and provides a description of what is in it. This description is important because it is what users see before they import a content pack to their workspace. You can also choose an image but if you opt not to, a default one is used instead.

The most important part of the dialog box is the section where you choose what is to be published. You will see three lists for the reports, dashboards and datasets in your own personal workspace and you can choose pretty much whatever you want, although there are a couple of constraints. If, for example you choose a dashboard, every dataset and report in the dashboard visualizations will be automatically included. The same goes for reports; underlying datasets are included automatically.

When Donald clicks Publish, his content pack gets published and shows up in the content pack lists that you can see in Settings>View Content Pack. Now, the other users within Donald's organization can use the content pack he created and, in the next part, we'll look at how this works and the difference between using existing packs and creating personal copies with the ability to modify them.

Using Organizational Content Packs

Susan can now use Donald's content pack. Clicking on Get Data makes Power Bi open the Get Data page. Susan goes to the Content Pack Library and then to My Organization. She clicks on Get and she can see a list of all the available content packs. There is also an option to create a new one. Right now, the only content pack that Susan can see is the one that Donald just published.

She clicks on it and the information Donald added at the time of publishing appears. She can see a content pack description, publisher name, and the time passed since publishing.

Susan clicks Connect and Power Bi imports all the entities from the content pack into her personal workspace. She sees a new dashboard on the left pane and a new dataset and report. She can navigate through the reports and dashboard in view mode easily and, if Donald were to update the content pack, she would automatically see the new versions. However, if she wanted to pin something on the dashboard, edit the report or create a new report in the dataset, she would immediately see a message asking her if she intends to personalize the pack.

If she removed any content pack object, every entity from the content pack will also be removed. If she continues with the personalization and clicks Save on the message, she would be creating a copy of the content pack objects and she can do what she wants with those.

Put simply, if Susan opts not to create a personal content pack copy, she will get any update made to it automatically but, if she does opt for the copy, she won't get the updates. She can do any modifications she wants in her copy but only with the reports and dashboards; modifications cannot be made to datasets because they are shared and the only person who can modify and refresh them is the owner.

Updating Organizational Content Packs

The content pack called Sales and Website 2017 is owned by Donald and, the second he publishes it on the Power Bi service, any changes made on the Power Bi service to any object will result in a special notification. If, for example, he moves the positions of the visualizations, he will get a message warning him that changes have been made to a published content pack and he needs to update it so others can see those changes. If he clicks the View Content Packs option on the message, he will see all the available content packs and he can see the ones that have been affected by any of his changes to the dashboards or reports.

Donald will see a warning icon beside the content pack he published and, if he holds his mouse over the icon, he will see the warning message. The owner of the content pack must update the changes for them to be automatically published as a new version. Donald clicks Edit, allowing him to publish that new version to replace the previously published one. The Update Content dialog box opens, almost identical to the Create Content Pack dialog box, with the exception that the Publish button now reads Update.

By clicking on Update, a new version of Donald's pack is generated and it will override his previously published one. When this is done, the objects in the content pack are automatically updated in the workspace of any user who has used that content pack before, without making any customizations. This all corresponds to the dashboard's share feature which, as you know, provides a copy of the dashboard, read-only, for others to see but can't make modifications to. However, when the content pack is used, it extends the capability to the datasets and reports, both of which may be in a content pack irrespective of whether they have been used in a dashboard or not.

If any person used the content pack and created a copy of their own, they will also see a warning message, this one telling them that there is a new version of the pack; nothing else will happen because modifications to the content pack are not published automatically to any of the corresponding entries in the users copy content pack. For example, Susan made a copy of the pack so none of the changes that Donald made to Sales and Website 2017 will show in her copy. However, she is using objects that were created from a newly updated content pack, she will get the warning message.

Now that Susan knows there is an updated version, she can make the decision as to whether she gets the data from that content pack again. If she does, she will get all the updated data imported into her workspace but the new objects will be named exactly the same as the original ones – for this reason, if you opt to copy a content pack, you should give the objects new names to avoid confusion if you reimport the same content pack again.

Summary

In this chapter, we looked at creating and using content packs in Power Bi. There are a few different content pack types, each having its own behaviors, available to users. We also saw how custom datasets can be created from services when corresponding service content packs cannot give you the data model you want.

These are the most relevant features:

- Content packs have datasets, reports, and dashboards in them; Power Bi users can import these straight to their own workspace and they can also customize the reports and the dashboards that are imported from the pack but they cannot customize the datasets

- You can only get content packs from the Power Bi service

- Service content packs are published by Microsoft; these can be used to make connections to services that import data used for populating predefined reports and dashboards. Credentials are required for the service you want to connect to extract the data

- Custom datasets can only be created in the Power Bi Desktop. You must use a connection that corresponds to the service content pack that you are not allowed to modify. Not all service packs will have that corresponding connector

- Organizational content packs may be published by anyone. They have predefined connections that go to data sources;

these cannot be modified by anyone other than the publisher of the content pack

- Content packs can be consumed or used just by reading the content or crating copies that can be modified

- The publisher can update content packs and the updates will be synchronized automatically with all those who use the pack as read-only.

Content packs are one of the most important Power Bi tools, helping you create predefined dashboards and reports based on the data that comes for an external service (already existing) or datasets created internally to the organization.

In chapter six, we are going to move things along a bit and look at building data models.

Chapter 6

Building Data Models

It's now time for Donald to move on to the next level in how he uses Power Bi. This could be considered as cheating a little but I really want this guide to show you what Power Bi is really capable of when you get to grips with it; I don't want to stick at just the basic features. We are going to assume that Donald has been impressed by the results he has seen so far so he has spent time learning about the DAX language and a bit about data modeling. . Having got some more information about Power Bi under his belt, he starts from scratch with the budget, this time having trust in his own knowledge of the tools available to him.

He loads the sales figures for previous years again but, this time, he ignores the view created by Kathy, the Corus database administrator. He opts to use basic views, atop the data warehouse, because they give him the data he wants but in a more fragmented manner. He has a table that has information about the stores, one with information about sales, one with the date and another that contains the actual products. With this information to hand, he starts by building a sales analysis project and ends by including all the budget information contained in the Excel workbook and prepares the dashboards using DAX code.

What I won't go into in detail are the code intricacies and formulas as related to the data model; one chapter is simply not enough space for you to learn about this. What I want to do is build the project so you can see the path that Donald takes – it is a basis for you to start your own Power Bi learning journey.

Loading the Tables

If you recall, in chapter three, Donald needed to get access from Kathy to the SQL Server database so he could see the view that shows him the sales for the last three years. Donald found out that there was a better way of analyzing sales – rather than the view Kathy gave him access to, he instead chooses to load his data from the original tables where the Corus information is stored. He gets together with Kathy to get some more details on how the Corus data warehouse is internally structured.

Kathy tells him the database has been organized into separate tables and he can access them using individual views, i.e. one for each table. In the database is a table for each individual entity within the Corus business:

Products – here Donald will find all the information he needs about the company's products

Sales – data containing detailed sales, with one row for each of the sales

Stores – contains information about the stores where the sales transactions take place

Data – a helper table with a calendar. When he attended a Business Intelligence class, Donald found out that tables like this are incredibly important for building good data models.

Kathy provides access to the views so Donald can load the information he needs. Once again, Donald opts to start over and opens the Power Bi Desktop. He loads all the tables into one new model, doing the exact same thing as he did to load Sales2017 view this time, though, he loads in four tables at a time.

Rather than loading the tables via the Navigator dialog box, it is far more convenient to go to the Home tab and click on Edit Queries under External Data. The Query Editor opens and Donald can rename the tables, getting rid of the CorusBi prefix on them.

When he closes Query Editor, Donald sees that the table is loaded in the model by Power Bi Desktop. The Desktop will also create relationships between the table. However, the algorithm that does this is by no means perfect and it misses some of the relationships.

Donald goes to the Navigation bar and clicks the icon for Relationship View, bringing up the model and spot that a relationship between the Sales and Data tables has not been created. This really isn't a problem because Donald can create that relationship; all he has to do is drag DateKey from the table called Sales to DateKey in the table called Date; the relationship is now in place.

Implementing Measures

As it is, there are still some adjustments to be made in the model. First of all, Donald hides every column that he doesn't want visible when the reports are created. To do this, he goes to Report View, chooses the relevant columns, right-clicks and selects Hide. He hides every column and key that would provide misleading data should they be summed straight.

As an example, in the Sales table are two columns called Quantity and Net Price respectively. Power Bi will, by default, offer to sum the values in Net Price and provide a summary. This is not correct; doing this would not take the quantities sold into account.

While Power Bi's default summarization works well with simple data models, it doesn't work for anything more complex, such as loading your data from a relational database where numbers are not stored in ways that they can be used in Excel workbooks. Instead, you need to use DAX measures. In DAX- speak, a measure is a script written using DAX syntax and, when you use a measure, you make it possible to write code and produce data models that are far more powerful.

To compute the Sales Amount, Donald decides to create a measure. He goes to the Fields pane and clicks on Report View. Then he right-clicks on the table named Sales and clicks on New Measure. A formula bar appears above the middle pane so Donald removes "measure" and inserts this code instead:

Sales Amount = SUMX (Sales, Sales[Quantity] * Sales[Unit Price])

On its own, this is a very powerful measure. In fact, now that Donald is taking his data from the data warehouse, he can use any of the available columns to slice the data, not just the ones he saw in the single view from before. As an example, in the Product table are two columns, Category and Subcategory, which can be used to perform a sales analysis for the different countries/regions.

When you have more columns to use, analysis of previous years' sales becomes quite interesting. The report will show how each brand contributed, in relative terms, to the category called Computers while, on the line chart, we can see how the sales behaved over a period of time. Different colors are used to highlight different years and, with this tool, Donald can get the answers to a few questions he has about the data, such as peaks in certain years.

Creating Calculated Columns

When you have more power at your fingertips, the requirements of your data model are typically higher. For example, with the line chart, we have the sales data for the last three years using different lines; this could be useful if we wanted to compare sales over different years but if, instead, you wanted an analysis of sales behavior for the last three years, it would be more useful to have one line spanning the years.

The problem we have here is that, in the Date table, we have a column named Month Name. If you take the year out of the legend, the sales are divided by month and not, as we want, by month and year.

What Donald needs is one column that shows him the year and the month together. The original database doesn't have this column but he can create it himself using one of two options. First, he could make use of Query Editor and add the new column into the data query or he could choose to create a calculated column.

In chapter four, we looked at generating columns using Query Editor so, this time, we will look at calculated columns instead. For Donald to create a new column in his table, he clicks on Modeling on the Power Bi Desktop ribbon, and then on New Column.

He adds these columns into the Date table by inputting the measures below into the formula bar:

Month Year = FORMAT ('Date'[Date], "mmm YY")

Month Year Number = 'Date'[Year] * 100 + MONTH ('Date'[Date])

In the first column, there is a short version of the month and year, kept short so it works for the line chart. We use the second column, with the Sort By Column feature, to sort the first column.

If Month Name is now replaced with Month Year as the line chart axis, the visualization you get is the one you want, as it shows the way the sales have behaved over the last three years.

When you build a report, you will normally want a calculated column in the mix so the visualization looks good. On occasion, the descriptions will be oversized and, in others, like this one, a column is required so a specific behavior can be represented. Power Bi is a great environment to model your data in while you keep the visualization in mind as your goal.

Using Measures to Improve Your Report

By using measures and calculated columns for your analyses, the only limit is your own imagination. For example, using a couple of calculations, it is possible to build a report with a bubble chart showing product numbers against margin, divided by categories. Each bubble size indicates the amount of product sold.

To build the report, the measures are quite simple:

NumOfProducts = COUNTROWS ('Product')

Gross Margin = SUMX (Sales, Sales[Quantity] * (Sales[Unit Price] - Sales[Unit Cost]))

All NumOfProducts does is counts how many products there are and provides an idea of the number of articles contained in the portfolio. Gross Margin, on the other hand, works out the gross sales margin by taking the cost away from the unit price and then multiplying the value by quantity.

Integrating Budget Information

Donald is, so far, very excited about what Power Bi can do for him. In fact, he is so excited that he has actually forgotten that his task isn't about sales analysis; it's meant to be about budgeting! This is a downside to using Power Bi; you get so caught up with looking into your data and analyzing it that you can easily lose sight of what you are meant to be doing.

It's time for Donald to get back to the job at hand. This time, he wants the budget information integrated. It is simple enough to get the data from Excel and Donald knows how to do this already. However, when he examines the data model he sees the first problem. The new table that has the budget data in it has no relationship to any other table.

This time, it is nothing to do with Power Bi not finding the relationship; Donald corrected this issue using drag-and-drop. No, what has happened here is that relationships cannot be created in this way. If Donald were to drag the CountryRegion to the Store table from Budget, he would get an error message telling him that the relationship can't be created and it may be because intermediate data is missing. In short, the suggestion is that an intermediate table could help solve the issue. First, though, let's just step aside and see if we can understand the issues a little better.

It is possible to create relationships between a pair of tables provided the column used in the relationship creation is a key in the destination table. Using the DateKey column, a relationship can be created between Sales and Data; this is because, in Data, there is a different value for DateKey in each row. For any column to be considered a key, it is a given that it must have different values for each of the rows. With a given date, the entire row can be uniquely identified in Date. In the Budget data model, CountryRegion is not considered a key in either the Store table or the Budget table and that means a relationship cannot be created.

There are several ways this can be solved, either using DAX language or the model. If you choose the model-based solution, you will find it easier to learn and it is the suggested way.

When a table is created with every possible CountryRegion value, CountryRegion will then be a key and then you can create the Budget to Store relationships. To do this, you need Query Editor or you can learn a new method – calculated tables. These are tables that use the DAX language and they can be stored in your model and used like you would any table. Go to the Modeling tab on the Power Bi ribbon and click on New Table. Type the following expression into the formula bar:

CountryRegions =

```
SUMMARIZE (
   UNION (
      DISTINCT ( Budget[CountryRegion] ),
      DISTINCT ( Store[CountryRegion] )
   ),
```

[CountryRegion]
)

Let's drop back in on Donald, see how he is getting on. When he creates the table, he uses the values of CountryRegion from both Store and Budget and, with the partial results, he forms a union. Lastly, he uses Summarize to give him a CountryRegion summary table. By doing this, Donald ensures that all possible values are represented, references by the Store or the Budget tables, in the resulting table.

Donald now has his intermediate table and can go ahead and create the relationship between CountryRegion and Store and then another relationship between CountryRegion and Budget. It is a technical table and these are only useful for propagating the filter from the Store to the Budget table.

What Donald has done here, from a technical point of view, is created a relationship of a many-to-many type between Store and Budget. The bridge table is CountryRegions and, to make sure it works as it should, Donald creates the measure below; this will return the budget sum:

Budget Amount = SUM (Budget[Budget 2019])

This measure can be projected onto a report that has CountryRegion, the budget value and the sales value. CountryRegion will slice Budget Amount and Sales Amount correctly.

However, there are no real meaningful numbers on this report. Because it doesn't contain a year filter, the sales are being accumulated over all the years being used and they are being compared with the budget and that only has the 2019 forecasts in it. This can be solved with one measure; this computes the 2017 sales amount:

Sales 2017 = CALCULATE ([Sales Amount], 'Date'[Year] = 2015)

By using Sales 2017 instead of Sales Amount, we can now compare the numbers.

The same techniques need to be applied to the other column in Budget, the Brand column. The DAX code isn't much different; only the column name needs to be changed to get a list of the brands:

```
Brands =
 SUMMARIZE (
   UNION (
     DISTINCT ( Budget[Brand] ),
     DISTINCT ( Product[Brand] )
   ),
   [Brand]
 )
```

All good but, with the next step another problem is hidden, one that requires some theory.

When a relationship is created between Brands, Budget, and Product, your model shows a relationship created between Brands and Budget but it is not active. An inactive relationship is one that is there in the model, but it isn't used in the automatic value filtering. So, this was the final relationship we created – why was it deactivated by Power Bi? Simple – if it remained active, our model would be ambiguous. Because of the inactive relationship though, the filtering isn't happening as it should and a report built using brands and countries/region will always have incorrect results.

Ambiguous models are data models that have several paths linking a pair of tables. All the relationships are bidirectional, which means that the filters will apply in two directions. So, what ambiguity is there here? Well, there are a few. For example, when you begin with Product, you can follow the chain of Product->Brands->Budget or the chain of Product->Sales->Store->CountryRegion - if every relationship was active, both of those paths would be legal and that leads to ambiguity.

This can be solved in most cases simply by stopping traversal of the path while maintaining the features of the model. For example, in the model we looked at, we don't need to have Sales filter Product or Sales filter Store. It is sufficient that, for both cases, the opposite direction works; i.e. the Product and Store tables can both filter Sales. To do this, just double-click on any relationship – the line that connects them – and the Edit Relationship dialog box opens. For bidirectional filtering to be disabled, Cross Filter Direction should be set as Single. This should be done to multiple relationships – Sales to Store, Sales to Product and the two relationships that link Budget with Brands and CountryRegions.

Once the ambiguity is removed from your model, once the right relationship sets are activated, your model will work exactly as it should. To test it, build a matrix showing CountryRegion and Brand both correctly filtering the budget.

Budget Reallocation

Budget numbers can only be right if they are sliced by country/region or by brand because this is the granularity the budget was defined at. If, however you were to add in a column that doesn't really belong to the Budget table, i.e. slicing by Color and Country/Region, the result would be incorrect. Let's say that you have a table showing the values in the United States for several colors. The top two, Black and Silver values are both identical to the total value of all the colors sold in the country.

What this comes down to is not the number being wrong but an inability to understand what is being computed. The cell value, for example, at the United States/Black intersection is showing the sum of the US budget for all brands that contain at least one black product. Some colors, like Silver and Black, are in just about every brand and that is why those two rows show an identical total to the grand total.

Obviously, this is not what you want to see. What you want is a budget showing figures related only to the Black products or the Silver products sold in the USA but this isn't what you get.

The problem here is that the budget for any specific color, we'll stick with Black, isn't in the workbook used as the data source. In that, all you have is a budget showing the products from the same brand. However, even if the number you want isn't in there, it can be computed with a similar technique to what Donald used early in this book when he sliced his budget by month and divided the resulting value by 12.

To understand this technique, we'll start with the matrix report of the sales and budget along with a chart that filters the data, showing only that from Corus.

How do you determine Black's budget value? By taking the total and using an allocation factor to multiply it. We compute the allocation factor by dividing the total Black sales in 2017 by the grand sales total. As such, we have a 0.2165 correction factor.

This technique will allow you to allocate your budget based on the previous year's sales figures. You take the seasonality into account along with any other factors that result in lower or higher sales for a given category, subcategory, or color.

The budget granularity is country/region and brand. If, for now you focus on brand only, the allocation factor can be computed using this measure:

```
AllocationFactor =
DIVIDE (
    [Sales 2017],
    CALCULATE ( [Sales 2017], ALLEXCEPT ( 'Product', 'Product'[Brand] ) )
)
```

Now, the Budget Amount code can be modified with the allocation factor being taken into account:

```
Budget Amount = SUM ( Budget[Budget 2019] ) * [AllocationFactor]
```

The result now shows you that the budget has been sliced correctly by Color, despite the fact that the original budget wasn't sliced in this way.

Up to now, our focus has been on Brand and this is a Product table attribute. However, our budget has also been defined at the level of Country/Region and this has to be considered when the allocation factor is computed. The final measures or formulas that you need are:

```
AllocationFactor =
DIVIDE (
    [Sales 2017],
    CALCULATE (
        [Sales 2017],
        ALLEXCEPT ( 'Product', 'Product'[Brand] ),
```

        ALLEXCEPT(Store, Store[CountryRegion]),
        ALL (Date)
)
)

Budget Amount = SUM (Budget[Budget 2016]) * [AllocationFactor]

The allocation has been done against 2017 the result will show you the measures of Budget Amount, Sales 2017 and Sales 2016 whereas, in Budget, the same Sales 2017 distribution has been followed by Sales 2016 is ignored because it has a different number distribution.

Summary

As mentioned at the start, we did cheat a little here because we didn't want to give you yet another step-by-step implementation guide. Instead we wanted to show you what Power Bi is capable of when you start getting into the more advanced tools.

The relevant features are:

- **Model Building** – when the raw tables are loaded from the SQL Server database and not using predefined queries that have aggregated values, the analyses you can do are so much more powerful. At the same time, you have full responsibility over the model building process and you can use all the tools that Power Bi offers to build more complex models

- **DAX** – DAX is the Power Bi language, a great aide when you want to analyze data. We used it for creating calculated tables, calculated columns, and measures although it is capable of so much more.

- **Columns for Specific Charts** – on occasion, you will need a column for one chart and all you have to do is build it.

With basic skills, you can go from using Power Bi as a reporting tool right up to its full potential – a very powerful tool for data modeling offering you the ability to use your data for truly useful analyses.

In the final chapter, we will look into how to improve your reports in Power Bi.

Chapter 7

Improving Your Power Bi Reports

Over the previous chapters, I have introduced you to lots of different Power Bi features, all related to creating dashboards, reports, sharing and publishing and data modeling, along with a very quick introduction to DAX, the Power Bi language. Although the story behind the book has been on drawing up budgets, it is important to remember that the focus is on the data, on how to do it and not on what the numbers are.

Donald took full advantage of everything we talked about here and he created the right solution for his budgeting reports, using Power Bi to create a fully collaborative environment for him and his team. Up to now, we have spent most of our time looking at data and numbers, not on the visuals. In this chapter, we are going to look at how to use visuals to improve how your data model dashboards and reports.

We'll be looking at different dashboards, different datasets and different requirements to show you Power Bi's tools and capability for visual presentation. We are going beyond the requirements Donald needed for his scenario; we need to look at a much broader scope.

You will learn how to make a choice between the visualizations built into Power Bi, how and when to use custom visualizations, how DAX can be used to fix common issues with reporting and, lastly, the approach you should be taking when you need to design a high-density report.

Please do not expect a full step-by-step tutorial on using the visual editor supplied in Power Bi; that is not what this chapter is about. Nor is it about providing you with a guide on the visual patterns, or all the standard or custom Power Bi visualizations. The idea of this chapter is to show what options you have in Power Bi; it is a basic guide to help you choose your visualizations, depending entirely on your own requirements.

To do that, I will be providing you with several different examples, giving you the reasons for the design choices, giving you the background you need to apply those same principles to your own reports.

Standard Power Bi Visualizations

Power Bi provides you with a number of built-in visualization options. You will also see, throughout this chapter, how to improve on these options by using a series of customized visualizations. Before we get into that, though, you need to have an understanding of how you can and cannot use the standard visualization components.

Right now, there are 27 standard visual components in Power Bi, but this is expected to expand with future updates to the service. These are the current components:

Stacked Bar Chart - used when you need a comparison between the different values, side by side, of the same measure. Can also be used when you have different measures, part of one whole, that you want to be displayed. The bars are horizontal.

Stacked Column Chart – this is exactly the same as the stacked bar chart but with a vertical orientation instead

Clustered Bar Chart – much like the stacked bar chart but, rather than different measures being compared in the same bar, they can be compared side-by-side. The clusters are horizontal

Clustered Column Chart – this is exactly the same as a clustered bar chart but with a vertical orientation

100% Stacked Bar Chart – much like the stacked bar chart but each measure uses one slice of each bar which must always correspond to the whole available width, i.e. 100%. The bars are horizontal

100% Stacked Column Chart – much the same as the 100% stacked bar chart but with vertical orientation

Line Chart – this is used for displaying measure trends over time. The y-axis normally has a range that excludes zero.

Area Chart – like the line chart, this is used when you have cumulative data that you want to display, rather than a sequence of points. The y-axis normally starts at zero and only one measure is included. It looks much like the line chart with areas that are layers of color

Stacked Area Chart – like the area chart but each measure is cumulated to the other measures

Line and Stacked Column Chart – this is used when you have measures that have different scales, like percentage or currency, or that have different ranges of values, and you need to display them

Line and Clustered Column Chart – much the same as the line and stacked column chart but clustered columns are used rather than stacked columns

Waterfall Chart - this is used for displaying cumulative data. Each value is highlighted for its negative or positive value. The first and last value columns normally begin on the horizontal access and color-coded columns float between them, hence the name, 'waterfall'.

Scatter Chart – this is used when you have two measures where you want to display possible correlations

Pie Chart – this is used for displaying the value distribution for one or more measures. Each measure is one slice of the pie with the larger values taking larger slices. Pie charts are not considered to be best practice

Treemap – like a pie chart but with a different representation. Colored rectangles are used to represent the values and it may be used as a pie chart alternative but, when it has a lot of elements it is just as unreadable as the pie chart

Map – this is used for displaying geographical data using different sizes of circles on a Bing map

Table – this is used for displaying data in a simple table as text; each measure and each attribute is a column

Matrix – used to extend a table so that measures can be grouped by columns and rows

Filled Map – like the map but with colored overlays used to represent the data

Funnel – like a stacked bar chart but it has only one measure and the graphical representation is not the same. The rows are stacked up in order which is why the chart looks like a funnel

Gauge – this is used to display one measure against one goal. The chart looks like a gauge that you might see in a car

Multi-Row Card – This is used for displaying multiple attributes and measures for each individual instance of a single entity. Each one is on a different graphical and colored card

Card – this is used to textually display one value (numerical) of a measure on a graphical, colored card

KPI – this is used to display one value using a background trend line chart; performance is highlighted using different colors

Slicer – this is used to filter at least one chart by choosing attribute values

Donut Chart – like the pie chart but with a graphical representation looking like a tire or a donut. As with the pie chart, this is not best practice

R-Script Visual – this is used to display charts that are generated using the R computer language

The first principle of design is the simplest one – you may have multiple components at your disposal but you don't have to make use of all of them. It would look incredibly confusing and messy if you had so many visual representations in one report. As such, it is not best practice to use too many in a single report without having a very good reason for it.

You may also find that the default properties of any given component may not suit your report and that is where modification comes in. Over the course of this chapter you will see a number of examples of the design principles, giving you more of an idea of how to use them.

For example, let's say that we a dashboard that displays the Corus Sales values. If you choose the right visualization and use the right colors in it, your data will be well-represented and whoever sees it will be focused on the data; get it wrong and all they will see is the mess you made of the visualization.

A good example would be to use just two colors, say black and yellow. Let's say that we have a report showing the sales amount, target values, and margin sliced by brand, dates, class, and subcategory. With just two colors in use, black shows the measure for the sales amount and those in yellow visualize the rest of the comparison measures which would be, depending on your visualization, sales cost, target, and margin percentage.

The visualization would show four charts, all using a limited number of the standard visualizations available – line, bar and columns charts. We will look at the reasons for choosing these visualization choices in the next part but, generally, it is best to stick to using simple visualizations that are easily recognizable when you are displaying understandable and useful information.

Choosing Between the Standard Visuals

The first chart is comparing the Target values and the Sales amount and it uses nothing more than a line chart. This is the main choice when measures are displayed over date or time ranges. The x-axis is always used for the temporal dimension. By using the Data color properties, you can choose the colors you want for each measure.

A variation of the line chart can be used when you need to display a measure that is part of another one. For example, let's say we are comparing the Sales Cost and Sales Amount measures. In theory, the Sales Amount should always be higher than Sales Cost and this margin is represented by a graphical distance. If you use a line chart, you may not be able to see that distance clearly enough so you can change things slightly; the area beneath the line can be 'painted' and this is done using the measure values along time – in other words, you can use an area chart.

The y-axis must start at zero; if it doesn't, the area cannot represent the two values correctly. A grey area is used to visibly express the delta in between those measures graphically and it is correspondent to the margin. If you have multiple intersections that go between different lines, an area chart should not be used. In fact, area charts should really only be used when you have measures that do not often intersect.

If you have measures that have different scales then you need to use specific visualizations. For a start, two y-axes are required, along with a way of associating the axis that corresponds to each individual measure. If you used both a line chart and a stacked column chart, you can show the measure for sales amount divided by class and category and compare it with the margin percent, also divided by category – this will show you more details.

The main measure here is the sales amount and the left y-axis is used to represent its scale. The right y-axis represents the scale of margin percent, which is the other measure. On the x-axis, you see the category name as it corresponds to each column and the category is divided, this time by class. Different grey shades are used to represent them. The x-axis is often called the 'shared' axis and more than one attribute can be included on it. In our example, two attributes were used, both for products – Category and Subcategory. Doing this gives us the ability to drill interactively down through the data.

There is a drill-down feature that you can activate for a column chart – click on the down-arrow icon beside the selected column chart. When it is activated, you will see the down icon, which is the drill-down icon show a black background.

Now, when you click any column in the chart, it is possible to drill down through every subcategory of the column. If you want to drill up through the categories, click on the drill-up button, which is the up arrow that you see in the top-left corner of your visualization.

When you have moved back up to the product category, by clicking the double-arrow that you see in the top-left corner, you can drill down to every subcategory of every category. By drilling down to the subcategory level for every category, you get a chart showing the Margin and Sales Amount percentage measures; because they both have the granularity of subcategories, they can be compared.

Using Custom Visualizations

While there are embedded visualizations that you can use in Power Bi out of the box, by making changes to their properties, you can have them represent your data more solidly. However, there may be times when you need your data displayed in a way that the standard components simply can't provide. Power Bi can help you there by providing a gallery containing custom visualizations. These have all been provided by Power Bi community members and you can download any of them for use in your reports.

In this section of the chapter, we are going to look at how you can improve your reports by using features found in some of the custom visualizations. The idea is to tell you how custom visualizations can be used in your reports and how they will improve things. There isn't space or time to cover every one of the custom options so, while I will cover a few of them, I would suggest that you go into Power Bi and have a look at the gallery showing all that are available now – more are being added every week.

Your First Steps with Custom Visualizations

So, our first improvement will be to a dashboard for Sales. There are no files for you to download to follow along with this so just keep up as best you can and use your own data to experiment.

The dashboard has the Sales Amount and the Margin Percentage and we want to give each a color as per their values. With the standard card component, each value has a fixed color and, while you can use the Data Label properties to change it, the choice is static. We want to change the color dynamically; this way, when the value of the Sales Amount increases by 20% or more over the previous year, it turns green. And, for Margin percentage, we want it to be green when it is over 130%, yellow when it is 100% to 130% and, when it drops below 100%, it turns red. You could choose to keep the red color for showing negatives in other scenarios.

To do this, we need to use a custom visualization that can change the color dynamically of the value on display, based on specific states. You could use the Card With States By SQLBI visualization from the gallery. When you have downloaded it, the file must be saved with the .pbivis extension, denting it as a Power Bi Visual file.

Going to the Visualization pane, click the Import from File button and import the newly saved visualization into your report.

If you have selected the card visualization that shows the Sales Amount, you can easily change it to the new one by going to the Visualization pane and clicking the new card button that showed up after you downloaded it.

In the component, go to the Fields pane and set the State Value so it reads YOY% - this measure is defined within the data model that has the year-over-year (YOY) growth shown as a percentage. If growth if negative, we want the color to be red; if it is positive and less or equal to 20% we want yellow and, if growth is positive and more than 20%, we want it to be green. Go to the State 2 section and set the To Value property as 0.2 – this is correspondent to an increase of 20%. Then go to the State 3 section and set From Value as 0.2.

The same operation is repeated for the card showing Margin Percentage; change it to the Card With States By SQLBI visualization, the State Value field should be set to the Margin percentage measure; in State 2 properties set To Value as 1.3 and in State 3 properties, set From Value to 1.3. By doing this, the Margin Percentage is displayed with the same value shown and Sales Amount will be shown in a color, based on the growth percentage, year-on-year. Experiment a little with your data, change the selection of categories, months, brands and so on and different colors will show up.

This is a simple example but it explains how to import custom visualizations and use them in your reports. Shortly we will be looking at how to determine when you should or shouldn't use custom visualizations.

Improve Your Reports

In the initial dashboard, one of the available charts is the clustered bar chart and it shows what the sales amount is divided by brand. Like all the other charts, this is updated dynamically when a month is selected, or an element in another chart that is in the same dashboard. It is for this reason that the displayed values correspond to those sales that the selections in the slicers and charts filter. That said, you might opt to compare the amount of sales per brand with the sales made 12 months before, as well as with the defined goal for each of the selections.

If you have other measures you want to display in the chart, they must be added. Each will have its own bar and you should choose a different color to differentiate the measures.

You could also think about using another type of visualization to make the chart easier to read. As an example, if you used one called Bullet Chart By SQLBI you could have the sales amount for 2018 as one bar in the center and a shorter bar, overlapping and surrounding it, to show the sales amount for 2017. And a short, vertical line is a goal value marker. The use of different graphics in one chart makes it easier for viewers to see what the most important value is and how the values are compared.

Another example would be a report that shows the population density in each US state using one of the standard visualizations, the filled map. Dark shades represent high-density and light shades represent low density.

What the visualization doesn't show is the names of the States because over 95% of them have been condensed into less than 20% of the chart's available real estate so there isn't enough room.

The same information could be represented with a custom map; states could be moved to different positions and their sizes changed so the map becomes easier to read. The custom visual for this is called Synoptic Panel By SQLBI and t will allow you to draw custom areas on maps.

With the Synoptic Panel visualization and the custom map of the US, you can create a map that shows each State, named, along with a shade of grey to represent its density. As well as that, this visualization works offline where the standard one needs you to be connected to the internet as the Bing Map service needs to be queried.

Again, this section has given you some ideas on how to use custom visualizations to improve your reports. Up to now, standard visualization components have been sufficient to show our data and custom visualizations have just made the process that much better.

When Custom Visualizations are needed

This time, we are going to use another report to look at conditions where visualization choices may be better or worse in terms of meaningful results. We're going to consider a report showing a stocks portfolio; charts are used to show historical stock prices and to show the way different shares behave, individually and as part of the portfolio.

The current report shows each stock represented by a line chart, showing the closing price of the ticker corresponding to it. The portfolio details are shown in a table in the top-left corner, showing how much of each stock is owned and its value, using the current stock prices. A line chart also represents the whole portfolio, where each stock is represented by a different colored line. That line is representing the total stock value over time. This is a useful chart for identifying the stock that has the biggest value over time in the portfolio. However, what it doesn't show us the total value of the entire portfolio over time.

Each color is indicative of a different stock so you else get an idea of each stock's weight in the portfolio. The biggest difference between line charts and stacked area charts is that, in the latter, each stock's name accumulates in value but a line chart shows each individual stock name. This is a case where the right choice of visualization between those that exist can provide you with the best presentation.

The four charts used to display the daily stock prices don't give complete information. In the data model, there are different values for each day – the open price, the minimum price, the maximum price and the closing price. These values are normally displayed for each period being considered, in the case of this example, a day, using a candlestick chart. You can't get a candlestick chart as standard in Power Bi so this is a case where a custom visualization is needed. You could use the Candlestick By SQLBI, which will give you a basic visualization with four measures for each of the periods – Open, Close, High, Low.

As you can see, custom visualizations can provide some neat improvements to your reports and, on occasion, they are needed if you are to get the graphical result you want. However, you may still need to play around with the data model a little to ensure the attributes and measures are shown in the way you want, with the correct granularity and formatting. The way to do that is with DAX and that is what we are looking at next.

Using DAX in Data Models

So far, we have looked at a few examples of different visualizations, such as how to choose the right one for making your report look better. We looked at the best ways to set properties and how to install custom visualizations when you need them. However, there are still improvements you can make that don't need any direct action on your visualizations. We mentioned earlier int eh book about creating measures and calculated columns using DAX. Normally, we use this to get a specific numeric result but there are times when you control the layout of your reports using DAX expressions.

In our first example, we look at the measures in the candlestick charts for the stock prices. Each of the displayed time periods has four measures – Open, Close, High, and Low. The data that has been stored in the data model has four columns that correspond to these for each stock and each day. However, the candlestick chart doesn't only have to be displayed by day; it can also be displayed by week or by month. The aggregation needed for each of the measures will depend entirely on the measure. For example, the price for the Open measure has to be value for DayOpen for the period's first day. And the price of the Close measure has to be the value for DayClose for the period's last day. The High measure price must be DayHigh's maximum value for the period while the Low measure price has to be the minimum. These four measures can be written using these DAX expressions:

```
Open =
IF (
    HASONEVALUE( StocksPrices[Date] ),
    VALUES ( StocksPrices[DayOpen] ),
    CALCULATE ( VALUES ( StocksPrices[DayOpen] ),
FIRSTDATE ( StocksPrices[Date] ) )
)

Close =
IF (
    HASONEVALUE( StocksPrices[Date] ),
    VALUES ( StocksPrices[DayClose] ),
    CALCULATE ( VALUES ( StocksPrices[DayClose] ),
LASTDATE ( StocksPrices[Date] ) )
)

High = MAX ( StocksPrices[DayHigh] )

Low = MIN ( StocksPrices[DayLow] )
```

It is, at times, a useful idea to create a measure for the purpose of displaying another measure that has a different name. The reason for this that many of the visualization components make use of the name of the measure in descriptions or legends and there is no way of renaming it with the visualization properties. For example, let's say that you have two measures named Current and Previous. What you want to display is the exact year in a specific visualization so you could create a pair of measures that have the year you want to be displayed in the legend. DAX code would look like this:

[2017] = [Previous]

[2018] = [Current]

To create the report, we extract data from Google Analytics. In the table called Website, there are two columns names Country ISO Code and Users. It would be cool if, in our dashboard, we could have a map that showed the ration between visitors to a website and the country/region population for those users. The population data can be imported into a separate table called COUNTRIES/Regions and then the Country ISO Code column used for linking it to the Website table.

The ration is going to be a decimal number so a metric could be created called Users Per Million. This would be created using the DAX measure definition:

```
Users per Million =
DIVIDE (
   SUM ( 'Website'[Users] ),
   SUM ( 'Countries'[Population] )
) * 1000000
```

Don't expect that a visualization component would do a ratio or a difference calculation, for example, directly. It is best for the corresponding calculation to be defined in a DA measure, which is then bound to the visualization.

Lastly, it is worth considering the use of a calculated column for classification that the existing data in a group, with a high level of granularity to the low number of values (unique ones) is much easier to show in a chart. For example, take the data values for a column called Browser Size, where the values come from Google Analytics. Browser Sizes come in over 5,000 different combinations of height and width; the fact that the values are so fragmented makes it hard to do the analysis. And, each of the browser resolutions is one string. Your reports need to group all the different resolutions using width and not height.

This problem can be divided down into two separate steps. The first step is to get the size of the width from the string; the digits that come before the x character in an integer are converted. Next, the number is compared with a list showing predefined values that represent the resolution range you want to be analyzed. The two calculations can be implemented using the following Dax measures, called Width Size and Width Category:

Width Size =
VAR xPos = FIND ("x", Website[Browser Size], , 0)
VAR widthString = IF (xPos > 1, LEFT (Website[Browser Size] , xPos - 1), "")
RETURN IF (widthString <> "", INT (widthString))

Width Category =

```
SWITCH (
    TRUE(),
    Website[Width Size] <= 1024, 1024,
    Website[Width Size] <= 1280, 1280,
    Website[Width Size] <= 1440, 1440,
    Website[Width Size] <= 1920, 1920,
    Website[Width Size] <= 2560, 2560,
    CALCULATE ( MAX ( Website[Width Size] ), ALL ( Website
) )
)
```

Creating A High-Density Report

To finish, not just this chapter, the whole book I want to talk about the challenges that come with high-density reports. When you have a lot of visualizations in one report, the amount of information that needs to be provided for each visualization must be balanced carefully. You need to remove any elements that are not necessary to the report, that would do nothing more than take the viewer's attention away from what is important. The idea is to have a viewer focus only the important data and, as you will come to see, it is far more important to have an idea of each visualizations tuning properties and structure than it is to use a specific custom visualization.

Let's take the first version of a report as an example; it contains website data obtained from Google Analytics and it for a website called DAX Formatter. In the report are 28 different visualizations, each one with data, and there is also one slicer and eight more visualizations that have no data; they are purely there for aesthetics and are the Title, Logo, Pictures, and the separators. The 28 visualizations cover just 7 different types of visualization, some of them being very simple variations on the same concepts – stacked and clustered bar and column charts. It is perfectly possible to create a highly complex report using just a few relevant visualization types.

The whole report has been organized into three different zones – center, left, and right. In the left one are the metrics that relate to how many users there are; in the center one is the data regarding the browsing sessions, and in the right one is some technical information – the average time for page-loading, type of device, operating system, browser used, and the resolution. If you wanted to create a report like this starting from scratch, the guidelines listed below would need to be applied:

Reduce the text - use only the minimum number of textual elements that are absolutely necessary – avoid the use of verbose and repetitive descriptions

Remove legends – where you can, leave legends out, particularly when you only have one measure in your chart

Remove axes – if the data labels are already included in a compact visualization, the corresponding axes can be removed. Clustered bar charts in particular should be formatted like this.

Use images where possible – if you are explaining a concept, try to use meaningful images or icons that relate to your data – they tell a story that would take far too many words.

We used a donut chart for the report; remember that we told you, right at the start, that pie charts and donut charts are not good practice so avoid them where you can. However, we wanted to include an exception in the chart – the comparison of just two values. The donut chart was used to display the distribution of the search engines, showing what percentage of the sessions came from Google and which from Bing. The Google searches are clearly in the lead when it comes to sending visitors to the website and Bing shows just a small contribution. For this, it isn't relevant to look at the exact percentage or number.

We want to improve three visualizations, starting with this example. Simple line charts are used as the spark lines on the report; they have no legend, no axes, no border, and no data label. And most of the formatting properties for the line charts have been set to Off.

What you cannot change is the line chart's line width. When line charts are used in small areas the result produced is not easy to read. You can use the Sparkline custom visualization to replace the line chart, downloading it from the gallery in Power Bi. Using this will give you a line that is smaller in width and the result is far easier to read.

We can also improve the countries/region penetration visualization. Rather than a standard map, which would have a pie chart for every country/region, its size being dependent on the density of the population, you can download the Synoptics Design panel, which loads the map of the world from the Power Bi Gallery. The result shows the measure for users per million.

The final visualization we can improve is the one showing the session numbers by browser resolution. The original data contains a fragmented number of some different resolutions and the bar chart displays just the first values. However, the number of sessions shown for the commonest resolutions is only 5% of all the sessions so a huge range of resolutions is considered and most of them cannot be seen in the report.

It took two steps to solve this. First off, we created a column that had the width category in it, used for classification of the width that was pulled from the resolution string. Next, the clustered bar chart was changed for a waterfall chart and, instead of the Sessions measure, we used the Sessions Percentage measure.

The waterfall chart does not contain a decreasing step but it is clear that the result easily shows a meaningful view of the resolution distribution. We created the Sessions Percentage measure as a DAX expression, like this:

Sessions % =
 DIVIDE (
    SUM (Website[Sessions]),

```
CALCULATE (
    SUM ( Website[Sessions] ),
    ALL ( Website[Width Category] )
  )
)
```

Once the improvements have been integrated, the overall difference can be seen in the result as an incremental improvement rather than a large change that we saw in the first instance when we used the standard components.

It is important, particularly in high-density reports that you focus on readability and quality, cutting out anything that isn't necessary and may distract the report user. High-density reports already contain a lot of information and the users do not need to be overwhelmed even more – keep your focus on data, on keeping it simple, and not on complicated visualizations and decorations that don't add anything.

Summary

In this last chapter, we looked at a few ways to improve your Power Bi reports. We looked at standard visualizations built into Power Bi and we looked at custom ones. The relevant steps are:

Choosing the right type of visualization – there are lots of built-in customizations that you can choose from but you shouldn't use too many in a single report. There is nothing wrong with using the same type in multiple reports if it works out the best way to show your data.

Customize the visualization properties – every visualization contains format properties you can change to customize them. For example, keeping a color scheme consistent is important in any good report.

Use custom visualizations when you need to – there are quite a few custom visualizations that you can use in the Power Bi gallery, great for extending the standard ones. These should be used only when they provide an advantage over using the standard ones.

Conclusion

Thank you for taking the time to read "Power Bi: A Complete Step by Step Beginners Guide to Understanding Power Bi". I hope that you found it useful and gained a lot from it.

Because Power Bi is not just one tool, I introduced many different concepts in the guide. You learned:

What Power Bi is and what it can do

How to build a Power Bi dashboard

How to use datasets to get the information you want

How to use Quick Insights, reports, and natural-language queries to visualize your data

How to apply filters

How to share dashboards, data, and reports, within and external to your organization

How to publish reports for public consumption

How to upload data models and refresh them

How to build data models

What Power Bi Desktop is and how to use it

How to use Query Editor for loading data and building models

How to create content packs in Power Bi Service

How to create custom datasets

An overview of the DAX language for data analysis

How to build columns for your charts

How to choose your visualization type and customize it

How to integrate Power Bi with Microsoft Office

And so much more

We managed to cover quite a bit in a short space, but be aware that, with the DAX language, I was only able to give you an overview. To fully understand DAX would take a book of its own and going into too much detail was not in the scope of this book.

The Power Bi ecosystem continues to grow with new features being added by Microsoft all the time, not to mention features provided by other third-party groups. This guide is the tip of the iceberg, the start of what should be a long and fruitful journey for your organization.

Once you have read this guide and you understand the concepts discussed, you can take your learning further. There are plenty of online tutorials, courses, and other books that you can read on the subject, right up to the most advanced levels. Just keep in mind that the best way to learn a system like Power Bi is to use it and use it often. Don't be afraid to experiment; it really is the best way to learn.

Thank you once again for purchasing my guide; I would like to take this opportunity to wish you and your organization the very best of luck on your Power Bi journey.

References

https://docs.microsoft.com

https://intellipaat.com

https://medium.com

https://powerbi.microsoft.com

https://radacad.com

https://www.computerworld.com

https://www.guru99.com

https://www.innovativearchitects.com

https://www.nigelfrank.com

https://www.tutorialgateway.org

https://www.tutorialspoint.com

Printed in Great Britain
by Amazon